Water

Critical Infrastructure and Key Resources
Sector-Specific Plan as input to the
National Infrastructure Protection Plan

May 2007

Homeland
Security

Environmental
Protection
Agency

Water Sector Government Coordinating Council Letter of Agreement

The Water Sector Government Coordinating Council (GCC) is pleased to concur on the 2007 Water Sector-Specific Plan (SSP). This plan provides the overarching framework for integrating Water Sector critical infrastructure and key resource protection efforts into a unified program coordinated by the Department of Homeland Security (DHS). Through direct collaboration, the Water Sector Coordinating Council (SCC) and the Water Sector GCC were able to develop a plan that lays out a logical and workable framework for a strong public/private partnership that will help secure the Water Sector and the country as a whole.

The Federal and State members that compose the Water Sector GCC support the concepts and processes described in the Water SSP and are committed to working with DHS and other sector security partners to help achieve the goals established in the plan. This work will be appropriate and consistent with the authorities, resources, and programs specific to each of the departments and agencies which compose the Water Sector GCC.

Recognizing that the Water SSP is intended to be a living document, the Water Sector GCC also commits to continuing to work with DHS and the Water SCC to ensure that the plan is updated as needed. This collaborative effort will enable us to better focus the limited resources available for critical water infrastructure protection in the most beneficial manner. As approved by those on the Water Sector GCC who participated in the review of the final 2007 Water SSP, I, Debbie Newberry as Chair of the Water Sector GCC, concur on this version of the Water SSP on behalf of the Water Sector GCC.

This signed "Letter of Agreement" from the Water Sector GCC indicates concurrence with the final 2007 Water SSP.

Deborah Newberry, PE
USEPA
Chair, Water Sector Government Coordinating Council

Water Sector Coordinating Council Endorsement Letter

May 1, 2006
The Honorable Robert Stephan
Assistant Secretary for Infrastructure Protection
Department of Homeland Security
Washington, DC 20528
(via email)

Dear Mr. Stephan:

This letter is to endorse the final version of the water Sector-Specific Plan (SSP) and acknowledge that the Environmental Protection Agency (EPA) actively engaged the Water Sector Coordinating Council (WSCC) during the plan's development.

Furthermore, the WSCC thanks you and the EPA for being so responsive to our comments throughout the development and subsequent revision of the SSP. The SSP development effort is an example of the value and productivity that can occur when federal and water sector security partners leverage the National Infrastructure Protection Plan's (NIPP) sector partnership model.

It is the sincere hope of the WSCC that the Department of Homeland Security (DHS) and EPA will continue to utilize the partnership model on both future and ongoing security initiatives, including those under the direction of Homeland Security Presidential Directives 5, 7, 8, 9, 10 and 12, all of which influence the security and resiliency of the water sector.

Throughout the development of the SSP, the WSCC's SSP Work Group identified critical issues that the Council felt needed to be appropriately captured within the SSP. The inclusion of these issues, outlined below, was key to the water sector's support of the final plan.

The issues of critical importance to the Council are summarized as follows:

- The SSP places greater emphasis on actions and programs that address "response and recovery" as opposed to just basic "prevention."

- The SSP clearly defines that the process for prioritizing the sector's Critical Infrastructure/Key Resource (CI/KR) will go through a joint Critical Infrastructure Protection Advisory Council (CIPAC) Work Group comprised of members designated by WSCC and the Government Coordinating Council (GCC).

- When addressing the Vulnerability Assessments (VAs), per the Bio-Terrorism Act, the SSP clearly acknowledges that the sector has been proactive and compliant with legislative mandates by completing vulnerability assessments and revising emergency response plans accordingly. It also articulates that the provisions within the Act to safeguard and protect submitted data, are viewed as integral and valued parts of the legislation. The SSP emphasizes the positive changes that were brought about because of the Act. Specifically, utilities use their VAs to prioritize security and emergency preparedness improvements by incorporating prevention, detection, response, and recovery strategies into their design.

We hope the articulation of these issues helps clarify the Council's endorsement of the final SSP. In closing, the Council would like to express thanks to the EPA writing team, led by Curt Baranowski, for working diligently with both WSCC and GCC Work Group members to compose the individual chapters of this most important document while working under difficult time and resource constraints.

Sincerely,

Billy Turner
WSCC Chair

Lynn Stovall
Former WSCC Chair

cc: Curt Baranowski
James Caverly
Cynthia Dougherty
Benjamin Grumbles
John Laws
Debbie Newberry
David Travers
WSCC Members

Acknowledgments

The U.S. Environmental Protection Agency (EPA or Agency) would like to acknowledge everyone who contributed to the development and finalization of the Water Sector-Specific Plan (SSP). In accordance with the Department of Homeland Security's (DHS) National Infrastructure Protection Plan partnership model, EPA worked in close collaboration with our Government Coordinating Council and Water Sector Coordinating Council to develop this plan. The individuals identified below are either members or representatives of one of the councils and devoted significant time, energy, effort, and resources to assist EPA with its Water Sector-Specific Plan.

Erica Brown	*Association of Metropolitan Water Agencies*
Cade Clark	*National Association of Water Companies*
Jerry Iwan	*Connecticut Department of Public Health*
Adam Krantz	*National Association of Clean Water Agencies*
John Laws	*Department of Homeland Security*
Kevin Morley	*American Water Works Association*
Bridget O'Grady	*Association of State Drinking Water Administrators*
Roy Ramani	*Water Environment Research Foundation*
Chris Rayburn	*American Water Works Association Research Foundation*
Ann Speisman	*U.S. Army Corps of Engineers/Washington Aqueduct*
Lynn Stovall	*Water Sector Coordinating Council/Greenville (SC) Water System*
Vance Taylor	*Association of Metropolitan Water Agencies*
Billy Turner	*Water Sector Coordinating Council/Columbus (GA) Water Works*

Special recognition is also given to those who reviewed, commented, and worked on the plan.

Curt Baranowski	U.S. Environmental Protection Agency
Paul Bennett	New York City Department of Environmental Protection
Tommy Brown	Department of Homeland Security
Tom Curtis	American Water Works Association
Paula Dannenfeldt	National Association of Clean Water Agencies
Shelly Foston	Meridian Institute
Michael Gritzuk	Pima County (AZ) Wastewater Management Department
Genevieve Hanson	Computer Sciences Corporation
Thomas Jacobus	U.S. Army Corps of Engineers/Washington Aqueduct
Colonel Art Kaminski	Office of the Secretary of Defense
William Komianos	American Water
Vanessa Leiby	The Cadmus Group
Debbie Newberry	U.S. Environmental Protection Agency
Scott Para	United Water Management and Services Company
Dave Paris	Manchester (NH) Water Works
Greg Spraul	U.S. Environmental Protection Agency
David Travers	U.S. Environmental Protection Agency
Emily Washington	The Cadmus Group

Table of Contents

List of Figures

List of Tables

Executive Summary

There are approximately 160,000 public drinking water utilities and more than 16,000 wastewater utilities in the United States. About 84 percent of the U.S. population receives its potable water from these drinking water utilities and more than 75 percent has its sanitary sewage treated by these wastewater utilities. The drinking water and wastewater sector (Water Sector) is vulnerable to a variety of attacks, including contamination with deadly agents and physical and cyber attacks. If these attacks were to occur, the result could be large numbers of illnesses or casualties or denial of service that would also affect public health and economic vitality. Critical services such as firefighting and health care (hospitals), and other dependent and interdependent sectors such as energy, transportation, and food and agriculture, would suffer negative impacts from a denial of Water Sector service. In collaboration with the entire sector, a broad-based strategy to address security needs is being implemented. This work includes providing support to utilities by preparing vulnerability assessment and emergency response tools, providing technical and financial assistance, and exchanging information. Each section of the Water Sector-Specific Plan (SSP), as defined by the Department of Homeland Security (DHS) in its 2006 Sector-Specific Plan Guidance, is described below.

1. Sector Profile and Goals

This section of the SSP provides an overview of the Water Sector. Each drinking water or wastewater utility is considered an asset that comprises many components. The discussion includes an explanation of the Environmental Protection Agency's (EPA's) relationships, as the Sector-Specific Agency (SSA), with the private sector, State and local agencies, other Federal departments and agencies, and the public; a description of the relevant Water Sector authorities; a summary of its vision and goals; and explanation of its value proposition.

Authorities. Implementation of the Safe Drinking Water Act (SDWA); Federal Water Pollution Control Act, or Clean Water Act (CWA); and other environmental regulatory authorities builds on long-established protective programs in the Water Sector to protect human health and the environment. A number of governing authorities pertain to the Water Sector; most provide broad environmental authority that may support security-related activities and initiatives. Other authorities directly address homeland security and affect the Water Sector, such as the Public Health Security and Bioterrorism Preparedness and Response Act of 2002 (Bioterrorism Act) and Homeland Security Presidential Directives (HSPDs) 5, 7, 8, 9, and 10.

Water Sector Security Partners. A variety of entities—including all levels of government and the public and private sectors—play roles in helping to secure each of the Nation's critical infrastructure and key resources (CI/KR) sectors. These entities often are referred to as Water Sector security partners. As the SSA for the Water Sector, EPA will continue to collaborate and build upon existing relationships with all parties in the sector: public and private drinking water and wastewater utilities; the Water Sector Coordinating Council (WSCC); the Government Coordinating Council (GCC); national and State associations; State, local, and tribal governments; research foundations; and other Federal agencies such as the DHS. This collaboration will enable EPA to better understand dependencies and interdependencies within and across sectors, develop tools and training, improve information-sharing and exchange mechanisms, and conduct research to make certain the owners and operators of critical Water Sector infrastructure are better able to prevent, detect, respond to, and recover from terrorist attacks, other intentional acts, natural disasters, and other hazards.

Sector Security Vision and Goals. The Water Sector's security goals outline the comprehensive protective posture that the government and infrastructure owner/operators are striving toward. EPA and a joint working group of the WSCC and GCC have collaborated to develop a vision statement and security goals that provide clear direction for CI/KR protection efforts.

Vision Statement for the Water Sector

The Water Sector's Security Vision is a secure and resilient drinking water and wastewater infrastructure that provides clean and safe water as an integral part of daily life. This Vision assures the economic vitality of and public confidence in the Nation's drinking water and wastewater through a layered defense of effective preparedness and security practices in the sector.

From the vision statement, the Water Sector has developed four goals that will drive development of protective programs and measures of success. These goals are: (1) sustain protection of public health and the environment; (2) recognize and reduce risks; (3) maintain a resilient infrastructure; and (4) increase communication, outreach, and public confidence.

Value Proposition. This section of the SSP identifies and discusses the benefits of efficiently and effectively securing the physical, human, and cyber elements of the Water Sector.

2. Identify Assets, Systems, Networks, and Functions

This section of the SSP discusses ongoing efforts by government agencies and Water Sector security partners to help the DHS identify, prioritize, and coordinate key sector resources and assets that could, if compromised, result in economic or public health impacts. The discussion includes a determination of the sector's relevant information parameters; an outline of data sources that help it manage risk and protect infrastructure assets; an evaluation of methods for verifying infrastructure information; and a review of methods for updating that information. The section explores the distinct roles and responsibilities of EPA, the DHS, and public and private sector owner/operators for risk assessment procedures and maintenance of asset databases.

Defining Information Parameters. The Water Sector is composed of a diverse set of drinking water and wastewater utilities. Characteristics of these utilities that are useful for defining sector infrastructure information are available in databases that EPA currently maintains. Drinking water and wastewater assets are defined as entire utilities for purposes of identification, prioritization, and coordination in the Water Sector. Owner/operators are responsible for conducting risk assessments of their utilities to identify asset components, (e.g., pumps, generators, and supervisory control and data acquisition systems) loss or damage of which, due to manmade or natural events, could adversely affect the utility's operation, threaten public health or the environment, or have significant economic impacts. Also provided are drinking water and wastewater categories common to the industry and that should be reflected in the DHS's National Asset Database (NADB).

Collecting Infrastructure Information. In coordination with the Water Sector, EPA maintains several databases that contain general information on drinking water and wastewater utilities. These databases are important in identifying, describing, and quantifying information about the sector. As part of its mission under the SDWA and CWA, EPA maintains general information about its inventory of regulated utilities, which is regularly updated by the States. This section also describes the Bioterrorism Act and the requirement for drinking water utilities serving more than 3,300 persons to conduct vulnerability assessments and provide this information to EPA. In addition, the DHS maintains and is enhancing a comprehensive catalog that includes an inventory and descriptive information about the assets and systems that comprise U.S. critical infrastructure. The NADB allows analysis of consequences, specific and common vulnerabilities, dependencies, and interdependencies within and across sectors and geographic regions.

Verifying Infrastructure Information. Much of the existing data collected by EPA that pertains to the Water Sector are subject to verification and validation protocols. EPA databases and surveys have well-established quality control and verification procedures for data collection and entry, including data screening, double-key entry, and logic checks. EPA audits State data at least once every 4 years using a formal audit process and data verification teams.

Updating Infrastructure Information. By virtue of EPA's approach to meeting its mission under the SDWA and CWA, two basic inventories for all Water Sector systems—the Safe Drinking Water Information System and Permit Compliance System—are updated routinely, and other databases are updated at least every four years. Where deemed necessary for the security of the homeland and critical infrastructure, and while recognizing resource and time constraints, EPA will work with the sector to ensure more frequent updates of data or data elements.

3. Assess Risks (Consequences, Vulnerabilities, and Threats)

This section of the SSP describes the Water Sector's approach for assessing risk, which is the measure of potential harm due to threat, vulnerability, and consequence. Risk as it relates to the sector is a function of the likely consequences of a disruption or successful attack; the likelihood and vulnerability of disruption or attack; and the vulnerability to a disruption or attack on drinking water or wastewater utilities or their components. This section also provides information on risk assessment methods that are unique to the sector; how these methodologies address DHS's Risk Analysis and Management for Critical Asset Protection criteria; how risk assessments have been implemented in the Water Sector; the roles of the various partners in conducting risk assessments; and the limitations on providing information on the outcome of assessments to the DHS.

Risk Assessment. The Water Sector was involved in development of a number of risk assessment tools to help drinking water and wastewater utilities be better prepared to prevent, detect, respond to, and recover from terrorist attacks, other intentional acts, natural disasters, and other hazards. Because of the diversity of assets in the sector (e.g., size, treatment complexity, disinfection practices), a number of risk assessment methodologies were created and are used. These methodologies address the full range of utility components, including the physical plant (physical), employees (human), information technology (cyber), communications, and customers. This section also discusses the limits on using findings from the assessments.

Screening Infrastructure. This section discusses these issues and avenues for proceeding forward in developing screening mechanisms. In light of the large number of Water Sector utilities throughout the Nation and the limited resources available to address their security, it is neither practical nor financially responsible to perform comprehensive risk assessments at all facilities. Thus, as a precursor to in-depth risk assessments, the sector should explore the use of screening methods and begin to develop a process to define high-consequence assets.

Assessing Consequences. This section describes a number of consequences of concern and outlines a number of dependencies and interdependencies in the Water Sector and across other CI/KR. Among the factors to consider in assessing the consequences of any disruption of a Water Sector asset are the: (1) magnitude of service disruption; (2) number of illnesses or deaths resulting from an event; (3) impact on public confidence; (4) chronic problems arising from specific events; (5) economic impacts; and (6) other indicators of the impact of each event, as determined by the utility. The consequences that are considered for the national comparative risk assessment are based on the criteria in HSPD-7.

Assessing Vulnerabilities. This section discusses the various vulnerability (risk) assessments developed for the Water Sector. Vulnerabilities are the characteristics of an asset's design, location, security posture, process, or operation that make it susceptible to destruction, incapacitation, or exploitation by mechanical failures, natural hazards, and terrorist attacks or other malicious acts. They are weaknesses that could result in consequences of concern, taking into account intrinsic structural weaknesses, protective measures, resiliency, and redundancies.

Assessing Threats. This section discusses the need for improved threat data and better coordination with the DHS and law enforcement and intelligence agencies. The Water Sector views threat analysis broadly, encompassing natural events, criminal acts, insider threats, and foreign and domestic terrorism. In the context of risk assessment, the threat component of risk analysis is based on the likelihood that an asset will be disrupted or attacked. To assist Water-Sector utilities in conducting risk assessments, baseline threat documents have been developed.

4. Prioritize Infrastructure

In this section of the SSP, the DHS requests that the Water Sector describe the process for risk-based prioritization of its assets. As part of the national comparative risk assessment described in the National Infrastructure Protection Plan (NIPP), prioritization across sectors (in support of national protective efforts) is performed by the DHS. Sectors are being asked to provide risk assessment information in a manner comparable with DHS risk management efforts to better support the national assessment.

5. Develop and Implement Protective Programs

This section of the SSP discusses how the Water Sector develops and implements protective programs that are used throughout the sector, and focuses on efforts to identify, assess, select, and implement protective programs and on EPA's role in facilitating implementation of such programs. A protective program is defined as a coordinated plan to prevent, deter, and mitigate terrorist attacks on critical assets, and to respond to and recover from such attacks as quickly and effectively as possible. Protective programs guide infrastructure owner/operators on the most effective strategies for protecting their assets, including critical components, given the general classes of threats applicable to their system and their specific vulnerabilities.

Overview of Sector Protective Programs. This section provides a brief history of protective programs in the Water Sector and the impact of various HSPDs and the Bioterrorism Act in helping identify and define protective programs. Several key protective programs and initiatives that address the sector's vision and goals are discussed, as well as collaborative processes within the sector to identify gaps and develop programs.

Determining Protective Program Needs. This section describes the process EPA uses to engage sector security partners to identify and prioritize gaps and protective program needs.

Protective Program Implementation. This section describes the voluntary nature of protective programs in the Water Sector. It also describes the historical approach to protection, which focused on natural disasters and emergencies, and how this approach has been expanded to address security-related needs.

Protective Program Performance. This section describes how protective program performance changes and the need to focus on Water Sector goals and the highest priority security needs.

6. Measure Progress

Measuring progress is part of the NIPP risk management framework. While the DHS focuses on using core metrics to measure progress across all CI/KR sectors, EPA is responsible for measuring progress in the Water Sector using additional sector-specific metrics. In this section, the Water Sector describes how it will develop sector-specific metrics and how its partners will work together to collect, verify, and report requirements of the core NIPP metrics and of the sector-specific metrics. These metrics will be used to measure risk assessment progress and support continuous improvement in the Water Sector.

CI/KR Performance Measurement. This section describes the different types of measures that will be developed and the process EPA and its sector security partners will use to develop sector-specific metrics. It also discusses information collection and reporting.

Implementation Actions. This section of the SSP provides a matrix of various planned security-related actions, and the roles of sector security partners in development and implementation.

Challenges and Continuous Improvement. This section focuses not only on the challenges of measuring progress but also on other challenges faced by the sector in effectively implementing and measuring protective programs.

7. CI/KR Protection Research and Development

Many ongoing security-related research and development (R&D) initiatives have direct impacts on the Water Sector; other initiatives, while not directly related to the sector, can benefit its overall security posture. R&D initiatives are being conducted by educational institutions, national research laboratories, public/private research foundations, the Federal Government, and other organizations. This section of the SSP focuses mainly on the R&D initiatives being conducted by EPA's National Homeland Security Research Center, and on the center's coordination and collaboration with sector R&D partners. Also depicted in this section are the management process for implementing and maintaining research activities and how the sector's vision, goals, and R&D efforts align with the nine critical infrastructure protection (CIP) R&D themes and three CIP R&D goals outlined in the National CIP (NCIP) R&D Plan.

Overview of Sector R&D. This section describes the sector's technology development decision-makers and the process used to develop its R&D plan.

Sector R&D Requirements and R&D Plan. This section describes the sector's current R&D plan and identification of additional security-related research needs.

R&D Management Process. This section describes how the Water Sector will pursue a focused, coordinated approach that: (1) aligns the NCIP R&D Plan themes and goals with existing and future R&D initiatives and the sector's vision, goals, and objectives; (2) initiates specific projects to address critical needs; and (3) provides a mechanism for collaboration, project management, and oversight. The aim of this approach is to accomplish clearly defined activities, projects, and initiatives that contain time-based deliverables tied to priority R&D requirements.

8. Managing and Coordinating SSA Responsibilities

This section of the SSP details many of the management and coordination activities that will be performed in order for the Water Sector to better protect critical infrastructure.

Program Management Approach. This section describes how EPA coordinates security-related issues, its role as the Water SSA, and how it coordinates and communicates with the sector.

Processes and Responsibilities. This section describes the process for updating and maintaining the SSP, requirements for annual reporting to the DHS, resources and budget processes, and training and education.

Implementing the Sector Partnership Model. This section describes the NIPP sector partnership model, NIPP coordinating structures, and coordination with State and local government entities.

Information Sharing, Collection, and Protection. This section discusses the Water Sector's information-sharing mechanisms, and how information is collected and protected.

Introduction

We all rely on clean and safe water. Therefore, from the standpoints of public health and economic impacts, it is critical that we protect the Nation's drinking water and wastewater infrastructure, collectively known as the Water Sector. For decades, Water Sector utilities have been protecting human health and the environment. EPA has been working with its Water Sector security partners—public and private drinking water and wastewater utilities; the WSCC; GCC; national and State associations; State, local, and tribal governments; research foundations; and other Federal agencies—to better secure CI/KR across the Nation. This work began prior to September 11, 2001, and many of EPA's ongoing programs support security-related activities. All Water Sector security partners continue to collaborate to be better prepared to prevent, detect, respond to, and recover from terrorist attacks and other intentional acts, natural disasters, and other hazards (this is the "all-hazards" approach).

Under Homeland Security Presidential Directive 7 (HSPD-7), certain Federal agencies must identify and prioritize critical national infrastructure and resources for protection from terrorist acts that could cause catastrophic health impacts or mass casualties; undermine public confidence; or disrupt essential government functions, essential services, or the economy. In recognition of the distinctive characteristics of different infrastructure assets, HSPD-7 divides the national infrastructure into 17 CI/KR sectors and assigns CI/KR protection responsibilities for them to selected Federal agencies, called Sector-Specific Agencies (SSAs). HSPD-7 designates EPA as the SSA for the Water Sector.

A key requirement of HSPD-7 is that DHS develop a strategy to protect all CI/KR; that strategy is called the NIPP. It provides the unifying structure for integration of current and future CI/KR protection efforts into a single national program to achieve the goal of a safer, more secure Nation.

The NIPP follows the DHS risk management framework, which describes the processes for: (1) setting security goals for CI/KR protection; (2) identifying CI/KR assets; (3) assessing the risks to CI/KR assets, based on three factors: (a) consequence analysis, which is the SSAs' responsibility, with guidance from the DHS; (b) vulnerability assessments, which are the responsibility of the SSA and Water Sector; and (c) threat analysis, which is provided by the DHS, intelligence community, and law enforcement. The risk management framework further describes processes for (4) prioritizing CI/KR (as a basis for resource allocation); (5) implementing programs to protect CI/KR; and (6) measuring the effectiveness of CI/KR protection efforts. As part of the implementing structure for the NIPP, each SSA is to develop an SSP that follows and supports the framework. An SSP is the implementation plan of the strategy in a specific sector. Pursuant to the guidelines in HSPD-7, the NIPP focuses primarily on the terrorist threat to the Nation's infrastructure and resources. However, other hazards can affect the Nation's CI/KR as well, and are addressed in the NIPP and SSP.

The NIPP addresses relationship-building, information-sharing, resource allocation, R&D, and other processes that support implementation of the risk management framework on the national level. As figure I-1 illustrates, physical, cyber, and human elements of the infrastructure must be considered when implementing the framework.

Figure I-1: National Risk Management Framework

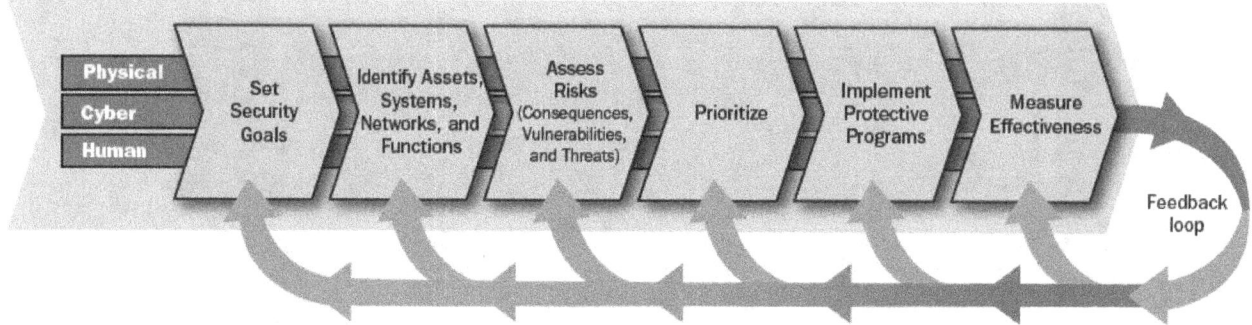

Continuous improvement to enhance protection of CI/KR

The Water SSP follows and supports the risk management approach and key steps outlined in the NIPP. This consistent structure facilitates DHS's cross-sector comparisons to foster coordination among security partners. The goal of the SSP is to describe and develop the Water Sector's strategy and programs to protect identified CI/KR assets, identify priorities and goals based on risk analysis, describe the resources needed to protect CI/KR, track progress, identify gaps, establish R&D priorities, identify best practices, and work with the DHS to continuously improve the NIPP. The Water SSP describes the specific processes used to identify, assess, prioritize, and protect CI/KR and to measure effectiveness. It also includes plans to implement these processes and the status of any efforts supporting implementation, such as best practices identified, challenges encountered, and products generated. The Water SSP also helps define the roles and responsibilities of EPA as the Water Sector SSA, and of others involved in securing the sector through implementation of the SSP. The processes and activities discussed in the SSP assist drinking water and wastewater utilities to be better prepared to prevent, detect, respond to, and recover from terrorist attacks, other intentional acts, natural disasters, and other hazards.

The NIPP and its SSP components provide the structure needed to coordinate, integrate, and synchronize activities derived from various relevant statutes and national strategies, such as the National Response Plan (NRP) and presidential directives, into the unified national approach to protect CI/KR. Relevant authorities include those that address the overarching homeland security and CI/KR protection missions, as well as those that address a wide range of sector-specific CI/KR protection-related functions, programs, and responsibilities. The connection between the NRP and NIPP is indicative of how these strategies work in tandem. The Nation's CI/KR protection efforts are based on ongoing coordination, cooperation, and collaboration between security partners for both steady-state activities under the NIPP and incident management activities under the NRP. The NIPP establishes the overall risk-based construct that defines the unified approach to protecting the Nation's CI/KR in an all-hazards context, and specifies the procedures and activities needed to reduce the risk to the Nation's CI/KR on a day-to-day basis. The NIPP depends on supporting SSPs for full implementation of the risk management framework throughout each CI/KR sector. Figure I-2 illustrates how overarching homeland security legislation, strategies, HSPDs, and related initiatives work together.

Figure I-2: Organization of Homeland Security: Related Authorities

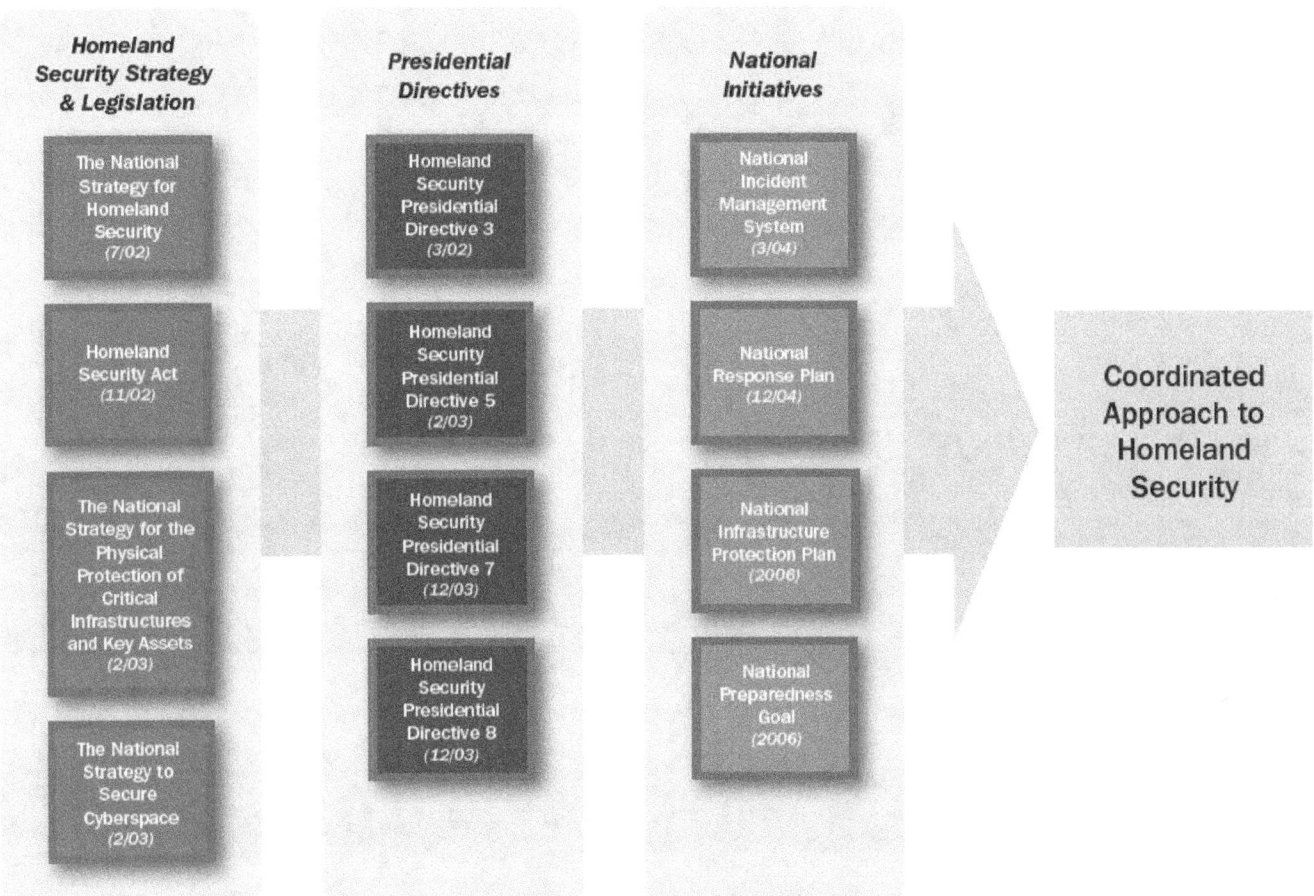

The multiyear NIPP describes mechanisms for sustaining the Nation's steady-state protective posture. The NIPP and its component SSPs include a process for annual reviews; periodic interim updates as required; and are to be reissued every three years, or more frequently, if directed by the Secretary of Homeland Security. The DHS oversees the review and maintenance process for the NIPP; the SSAs, in coordination with the GCCs and SCCs, will establish and operate the mechanism(s) necessary to coordinate these reviews for their respective SSPs. The NIPP and SSP revision processes will include developing or updating any documents necessary to carry out NIPP activities.

1. Sector Profile and Goals

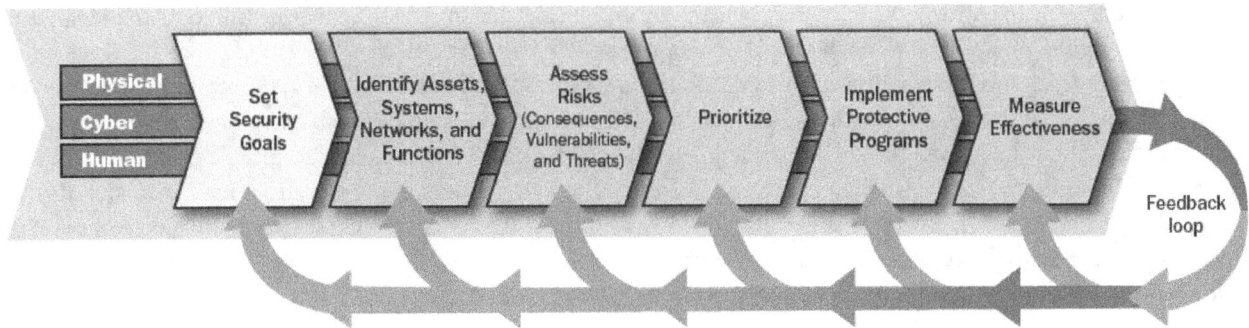

Continuous improvement to enhance protection of CI/KR

The United States has one of the safest water supplies in the world. The Water Sector, which comprises drinking water and wastewater assets, has a long history of implementing programs to provide clean and safe water, thereby protecting public health and the environment across the Nation. For more than 30 years, utilities have been conducting routine daily, weekly, and monthly water quality monitoring under guidance of the Safe Drinking Water Act (SDWA) and Clean Water Act (CWA), and researchers continue to explore ways to improve water quality testing methods. All of the sector's public health, environmental, and security-related efforts rely on a multi-barrier approach. For example, drinking water utilities typically employ a variety of protective programs that include source water protection, treatment and treatment redundancy, monitoring using certified laboratories, appropriately certified operators, and mechanisms to educate members of the public about water quality and inform them of any violations. Every community water system (CWS) must provide an annual report (sometimes called a consumer confidence report) to its customers. The report provides information related to the quality of the local drinking water, including the water's source, contaminants found in the water, and how consumers can get involved protecting it.

Because Water Sector utilities have always had to respond to natural disasters, emergency response planning is inherent to the industry. For decades, owner/operators of Water Sector assets have developed and improved plans to respond to manmade and natural disasters. Recently, either voluntarily or by legislative mandate, utilities have conducted risk assessments. Based on the findings of those assessments, owner/operators have created or updated emergency response plans (ERPs) and implemented security enhancements. These enhancements include:

- Improving control of access to utilities;

- Expanding physical barriers against vulnerabilities by installing equipment such as backflow prevention devices in pipes and locks on fire hydrants and manholes;

- Increasing control over access, delivery, and storage of chemicals;

- Hardening cyber network control systems by installing virus-detection software and firewalls, and in some cases by taking control systems offline; and

- Planning for operator and customer protection against influenza pandemics.

Non-Federal Water Sector security partners are traditional stewards of public health and the environment. Drinking water and wastewater utilities work to ensure continuity of operations to sustain public health and environmental protection. This concept is manifest in the sector's security vision and goals, in the need to be prepared for all hazards, and aligns with the sector's security culture.

The Environmental Protection Agency (EPA or the Agency) has a longstanding tradition of working through its 10 regional offices and with the 50 States, District of Columbia, tribes, and 6 Territories on oversight and implementation of regulations pertaining to the Water Sector. States play a particularly important role because of the drinking water primacy and wastewater permitting relationships the Agency has with them. Furthermore, EPA has developed relationships with local drinking water and wastewater utilities directly and through the national organizations that represent their issues and concerns. The Agency uses many communication vehicles and mechanisms to solicit input from Water Sector entities and to communicate regularly with the sector on a broad range of issues. It also has interacted historically with a number of Federal agencies to further its mission to protect public health and the environment. These interactions have been expanded to include other Federal agencies that play roles in source water, drinking water, and wastewater security. Several of these agencies have been identified as having critical dependencies and interdependencies with the Water Sector, and efforts are underway to develop communication mechanisms to share information and improve the working relationships among sectors at the national level. The relationships with these agencies and organizations are described more fully below.

These are only a few examples of what the Water Sector is doing to protect human health and the environment and to better prepare utilities to prevent, detect, respond to, and recover from manmade and naturally occurring events.

The water sector is one of 17 CI/KR sectors as defined by HSPD-7 and DHS. The Water Sector comprises drinking water and wastewater utilities in the United States. As the SSA for the Water Sector, EPA is required to coordinate the development of the Water SSP under the NIPP. The organization and content of the SSP is governed by the *Department of Homeland Security's 2006 Critical Infrastructure/Key Resources Protection Sector-Specific Plan Guidance*, issued in March 2006.

This section of the SSP provides an overview of the Water Sector, including descriptions of its profile; an explanation of EPA's relationships with sector security partners, other organizations, and agencies; a description of relevant authorities; and a description of the sector's security vision and goals. This section also describes the benefits beyond water security that the sector's actions may provide, including improvements to water quality and public health protection. Subsequent sections provide more details on identification and assessment of the sector's critical assets, as well as protective programs, research, and measures being developed to track changes in its long-term security posture.

In collaboration with its Water Sector security partners—public and private drinking water and wastewater utilities; the Water SCC; GCC; national Water Sector and State associations; State, local, and tribal governments; research foundations; and other Federal agencies—EPA has been working to better secure CI/KR across the Nation. Many of the Agency's programs and initiatives, as well as its overall mission of protecting human health and the environment, support protection of the Nation's critical drinking water and wastewater infrastructures. Presidential Decision Directive (PDD) 63, issued in May 1998, was a national effort to ensure the security of critical infrastructure across the United States. It established EPA as the national lead for critical infrastructure protection activities in the Water Sector. HSPD-7, which superseded PDD-63, was issued in December 2003. It designated EPA as the SSA for the Water Sector.

EPA's Water Sector Security Mission is to provide national leadership in developing and promoting security programs that enhance the sector's ability to prevent, detect, respond to, and recover from terrorist attacks, other intentional acts, natural disasters, and other hazards (the all-hazards approach).

As the SSA for the Water Sector, EPA will continue to collaborate with and build upon the relationships it has with all parties within the sector, with the Department of Homeland Security (DHS), and with other critical infrastructure sectors. The goals of these efforts are to better understand interdependencies, develop tools and training, improve information-sharing and exchange mechanisms, and conduct research activities making certain that critical Water Sector infrastructure and operations are not disrupted by terrorist attacks, other intentional acts, natural disasters, and other hazards.

In response to the September 11, 2001, attacks, EPA formed the Water Security Division (WSD) in the Office of Ground Water and Drinking Water. WSD oversees all drinking water and wastewater homeland security matters. The Office of Homeland Security (OHS) was created in the EPA Office of the Administrator to oversee all EPA matters related to homeland security.

On September 24, 2002, EPA announced formation of the National Homeland Security Research Center (NHSRC), headquartered in Cincinnati, OH. NHSRC is part of EPA's Office of Research and Development; it manages, coordinates, and supports a variety of research and technical assistance efforts. These efforts are designed to provide appropriate, affordable, effective, and validated technologies and methods for addressing risks posed by chemical, biological, and radiological terror attacks. Research focuses on enhancing the Water Sector's ability to detect, contain, and clean up such attacks.

The NHSRC provides a management structure that ensures effective design and oversight of research and facilitates interaction with EPA program offices and regions, other Federal agencies, the public and private sectors, and research partners. Its scientists and engineers are dedicated to understanding the terrorist threat, communicating risks, and mitigating attacks.

The Water Sector has developed the Water SSP to provide information on the activities and initiatives it is undertaking to identify, prioritize, and coordinate protection of critical sector infrastructure. This plan is divided into eight sections that focus on:

1. Sector profile and goals;

2. Identifying assets, systems, networks, and functions;

3. Assessing risks;

4. Prioritizing infrastructure;

5. Developing and implementing protective programs;

6. Measuring progress;

7. CI/KR protection research and development (R&D); and

8. Managing and coordinating SSA responsibilities.

1.1 Sector Profile

Safe drinking water and properly treated wastewater are critical to modern life. The former is a prerequisite for all human activity-physical, economic, and cultural. Wastewater treatment is important for preventing disease and protecting the environment. These extensive sets of infrastructure have been developed to ensure the protection of human health and the environment. Table 1-1 identifies a number of key statistics about the Water Sector.

Important to note, the term "asset" is used throughout the Water SSP to define each drinking water and wastewater utility. Water Sector assets are composed of numerous components, which are defined by owner/operators when they perform risk assessments on their utilities.

Asset = Drinking Water or Wastewater Utility

Because drinking water is consumed directly, health effects associated with contamination have long been major concerns. In addition, interruption or cessation of the drinking water supply can disrupt society, affecting human health and such critical activities as fire protection that can have significant consequences to the national or regional economies. The public correctly perceives drinking water as central to the life of an individual and of society. Consumers are highly sensitive to the threat of contamination or disruption. The Federal and State governments have long been active in addressing these risks and threats through regulations, technical assistance, research, and outreach programs. As a result, an extensive system of regulations governing maximum contaminants levels, of 90 contaminants, construction and operating standards (implemented mostly by the States), monitoring, emergency response planning, training, research, and education have been developed to better protect the Nation's drinking water supply and receiving waters. This regulatory system was created with active participation by Water Sector partners. EPA is using its position in the Water Sector and working with its security partners to coordinate protection of the Nation's drinking water supply from terrorist attacks, other intentional acts, natural disasters, and other hazards.

Disruption of a wastewater treatment utility or service can cause loss of life, economic impacts, and severe public health and environmental incidents. If wastewater infrastructure were to be damaged, the lack of redundancy in the sector might cause denial of service. The public is much less sensitive to the possible exploitation of wastewater infrastructure vulnerabilities compared to drinking water vulnerabilities. Regulations, research, and outreach, while extensive, have been aimed mostly at impacts to the environment due to service denials.

Table 1-1: Water Sector Statistics

Drinking Water
• There are approximately 160,000 public water systems (PWSs) in the United States.
• 84 percent of the total U.S. population is served by PWSs. The remainder is served primarily by private wells.
• PWS provide water for domestic (home), commercial, and industrial use.
• PWS produce 51 billion gallons per day (bgd) of drinking water-67 percent goes to residential customers and 33 percent to nonresidential customers.
• PWS obtain 63 percent of their source water from surface sources and 37 percent from groundwater sources.
• There are about 2.3 million miles of distribution system pipes in the United States.

Wastewater
• There are more than 16,000 publicly owned treatment works (POTWs) in the United States.
• 75 percent of the total U.S. population is served by POTWs; the remainder is served by decentralized or private septic systems.
• Approximately 27,000 commercial and industrial facilities rely on POTWs to treat their wastewater.
• 32 billion gallons of wastewater are treated every day.
• There are about 600,000 miles of publicly owned collection lines in the United States.

The next section describes the universe of utilities that comprise the Water Sector.

1.1.1 Drinking Water

There are approximately 160,000 PWSs in the United States, each of which regularly supplies drinking water to at least 25 persons or 15 service connections. These utilities are divided into community water systems (CWSs) and non-community water systems (NCWSs); CWSs that serve at least 25 year-round residents or 15 service connections to year-round residents. Examples of such systems include municipal water utilities and utilities serving mobile home parks or isolated residential developments. Non-community water systems do not serve a permanent resident population and are subdivided into two groups. The first-non-transient, non-community water systems (NTNCWSs)-serve the same populations of at least 25 persons at least 6 months of the year; examples include schools, factories, and churches. The second-transient, non-community water systems (TNCWSs)-include such facilities as roadside service areas, commercial campgrounds, hotels, and restaurants that have their own water supplies and serve transient populations at least 60 days per year. Water systems serving fewer than 25 persons or 15 connections, and privately owned wells, are not subject to SDWA regulation.

Under the SDWA, States can request primacy for their drinking water programs. Primacy gives a State the authority to oversee the program within its borders. To obtain primacy, a State must:

- Adopt regulations no less stringent than the national primary drinking water regulations promulgated by EPA;

- Have adequate procedures to enforce State regulations and conduct monitoring and inspections as required by Federal regulations;

- Maintain records as required by EPA;

- Adopt appropriate administrative penalty authority; and

- Adopt and implement a sound plan to provide safe drinking water during emergencies.

Forty-nine of the 50 States and the Navajo tribe have authority to administer their drinking water programs. Other sovereign tribal nations that do not have the authority have their programs regulated by the appropriate EPA regional office. State agencies that administer drinking water programs are known as primacy agencies. EPA Region 8 administers the drinking water program in Wyoming, which does not have primacy and EPA Region 3 administers the program in the District of Columbia, which does not have primacy.

Community water systems serve, by far, the largest portion of the U.S. populations. Based on Agency data from 2003, table 1-2 illustrates the number of each type of federally regulated drinking water system and how many people they serve. **Note that because many people consume water from both CWSs and NCWSs, the population-served figures cannot be added across types of system.**

Table 1-2: Public Water System Inventory Data

System Size		Water System Size Categories				Totals
By population served		≤3,300	3,301-49,999	50,000-99,999	≥100,000	
CWS	Total systems	44,764	7,756	476	367	53,363
	Population served	25,117,242	93,244,251	32,218,471	122,749,436	273,329,400
	% of systems	84%	15%	<1%	<1%	100%
	% of population	9%	34%	12%	45%	100%
NTNCWS	Total systems	19,569	114	1	2	19,686
	Population served	5,093,309	859,187	66,000	279,846	6,298,342
	% of systems	99%	1%	<1%	<1%	100%
	% of population	81%	14%	1%	4%	100%
TNCWS	Total systems	88,021	125	2	4	88,152
	Population served	9,911,753	1,050,772	103,700	12,269,000	23,335,225
	% of systems	100%	0%	0%	0%	100%
	% of population	42%	5%	<1%	53%	100%
	Total systems	152,354	7,995	479	373	161,201

CWS: Community water system. A public system that serves at least 25 year-round residents or 15 service connections to year-round residents.

NTNCWS: Non-transient, non-community water system. A public system that regularly supplies water to at least 25 of the same people at least 6 months per year, but not year-round. Some examples are schools, factories, and office buildings with their own water systems.

TNCWS: Transient non-community water system. A public system, such as a campground or gas station, that serves a transient population at least 60 days per year.

Active, current systems, from Safe Drinking Water Information System/Federal version, January 2004 frozen inventory table.

The distribution of CWSs by population served, however, is highly skewed, as shown in figure 1-1. The exhibit illustrates that, while 84 percent of the systems serve 3,300 people or fewer, they provide drinking water to only 9 percent of the population served by CWSs. By contrast, systems that service 3,301 people or more, and are required to conduct vulnerability assessments, provide drinking water to 91 percent of the CWS-served population.

Figure 1-1: CWS by System Size

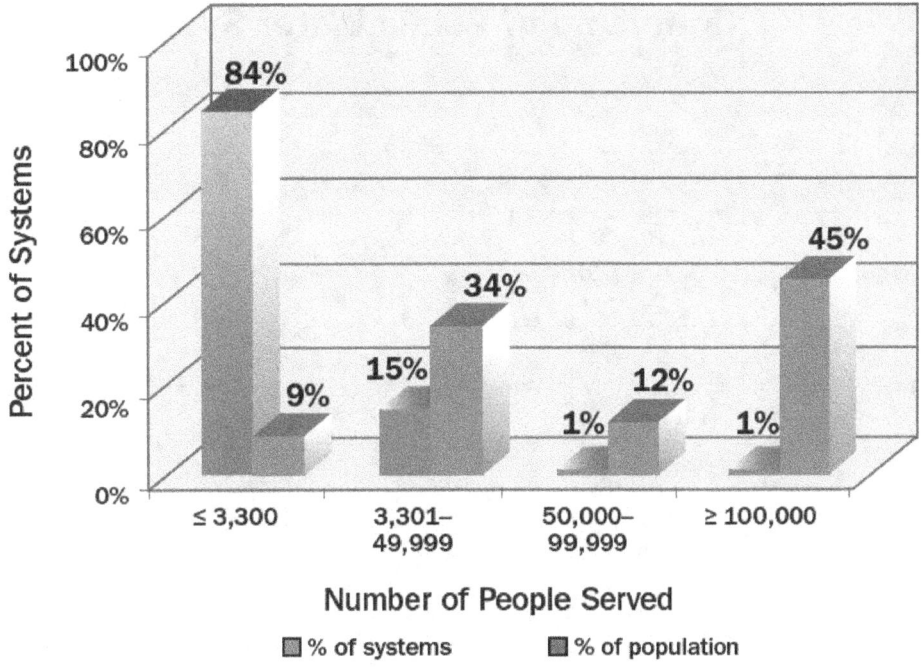

Figure 1-2 shows the ownership of public water systems by percentage and population served. The overwhelming majority of U.S. drinking water systems are publicly owned (by towns, cities, counties, or other forms of local government). Approximately 39 percent of privately owned systems, or 20 percent of all systems, are ancillary systems (that is, their primary business is not water supply, but they provide water as an integral part of their business). These systems tend to serve small populations, produce smaller quantities of water, and often do not bill customers separately for water. Most systems that rely mainly on surface or purchased water are publicly owned.

Figure 1-2: Ownership of PWS by Population Served

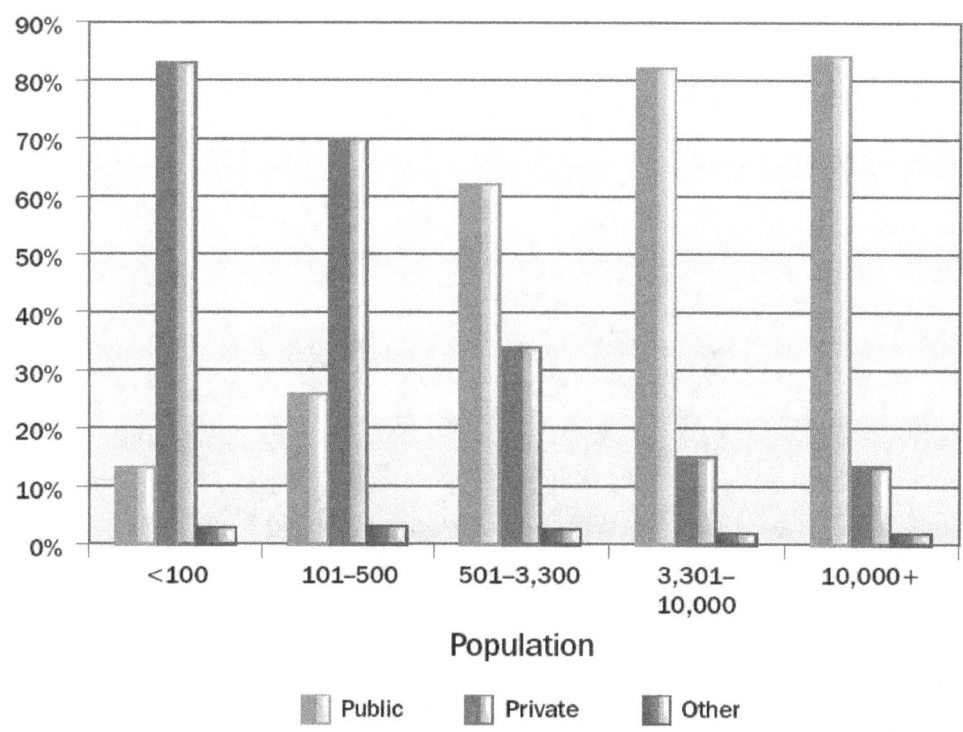

Ownership of Public Water Systems

Drinking water assets contain many components, as listed below. These are divided into physical, cyber, and human elements.

Physical

- **Water source.** This may be groundwater, surface water, or a combination of the two. The vast majority of CWSs serving fewer than 10,000 people use groundwater as their source. Large CWSs obtain most of their water from surface sources.

- **Conveyance.** To bring water from a remote source to the treatment plant, CWSs may use pipes or open canals. The water may be pumped or gravity-fed.

- **Raw water storage.** Reservoirs or tanks hold water from the source before it is treated. These reservoirs may be in remote or urban areas.

- **Treatment.** A variety of physical and chemical treatments are applied, depending on the contaminants detected in the raw water.

- **Finished water storage.** Treated water is stored before being distributed to customers. In a limited number of cases, treated water is stored in large, uncovered reservoirs that may be vulnerable to attack and contamination.

- **Distribution system.** This network of pipes, tanks, pumps, and valves conveys water to customers. The flow is adjusted so that the proper volume and pressure is delivered when and where needed.

- **Monitoring system.** Most monitoring is conducted for conventional regulated and unregulated contaminants. Some utilities have sensors installed at critical points to monitor a range of physical properties, such as water pressure and water quality.

Cyber

- **Supervisory Control and Data Acquisition (SCADA) System.** Some utilities have electronic networks, often including wireless communication, to link the monitoring system, and controls for the treatment and distribution systems, to a central display and operations room. These systems may also help to automate control of a drinking water utility with monitoring-system readouts serving as inputs for control. SCADA systems are part of integrated control systems essential to operation of drinking water utilities.

Human

- **Employees and Contractors.** Drinking water utilities rely on part-time, full-time, and contract employees to manage and operate their facilities. In larger utilities, this may include chemists, engineers, microbiologists, public relations people, security personnel, and other specialists who are highly trained in their roles individually and as a team. Operators must be appropriately trained and available, typically based on the type, size, and complexity of a utility. Utilities also rely on cadres of outside contractors to provide engineering services, laboratory analyses, chemical deliveries, and security services.

Drinking water utilities differ in the type of components used within each, and some utilities may not have all the components listed above (e.g., small utilities may not have SCADA systems).

1.1.2 Wastewater

Most wastewater is treated by publicly owned treatment works (POTWs), although there are a small number of private facilities such as industrial plants. The POTWs and privately owned wastewater treatment works that discharge treated effluent into the waters of the United States are subject to regulation under the CWA's National Pollutant Discharge Elimination System (NPDES) program. All but five States are authorized by EPA to administer parts of the NPDES program. In the five States that lack authorization, the appropriate EPA regional office administers the program. In either case, the administering body is referred to as the permitting authority. The permitting authority designates uses for all water bodies (e.g., fishing, swimming, and drinking), and then adopts water quality criteria that protect those uses. The permitting authority uses those criteria to set water quality standards for specific bodies of water. It then issues direct discharge permits that limit the concentrations of pollutants in the effluent, based on the water quality criteria appropriate to the receiving water body.

Private facilities that discharge effluent into a sewer system for subsequent treatment at a POTW are subject to the national pretreatment program. Many States are authorized to administer this program, which ensures that the private facility's effluent is compatible with the POTW's treatment capabilities or, if not, that the effluent is pretreated before being discharged to the POTW's collection system. EPA defines major and minor dischargers according to a formula that considers the type of industry, flow rate, types of pollutants, and other factors.

As of 2000, the following facilities were regulated under the NPDES program:

- Individual permits covered 16,255 POTWs;

- Individual permits covered 6,682 major direct dischargers;

- Individual permits covered 44,819 minor direct dischargers;

- General permits covered 43,586 minor direct dischargers;

- There were 1,482 pretreatment programs encompassing 22,538 major indirect dischargers ("significant industrial users"); and

• There were 835 combined (storm water and wastewater) sewer system permittees.

The distribution of POTWs by size and percentage of population served is shown in exhibit 7. POTWs with existing flows above 10 million gallons per day (mg/day) are considered large; there are about 533 of these utilities. POTWs with existing flows between 1 and 10 mg/day are considered medium; there are about 2,665 of these. POTWs with existing flows less than 1 mg/day are considered small; there are about 13,057 of these. For the purpose of determining population served, 1 mg/day corresponds to approximately 10,000 persons served.

Figure 1-3 shows that, while 80 percent of the utilities treat less than 1 mg/day, they provide wastewater treatment to only 11 percent of the population served by POTWs. Utilities that treat more than 1 mg/day provide wastewater treatment to the other 89 percent of the population.

Figure 1-3: POTWs by System Size

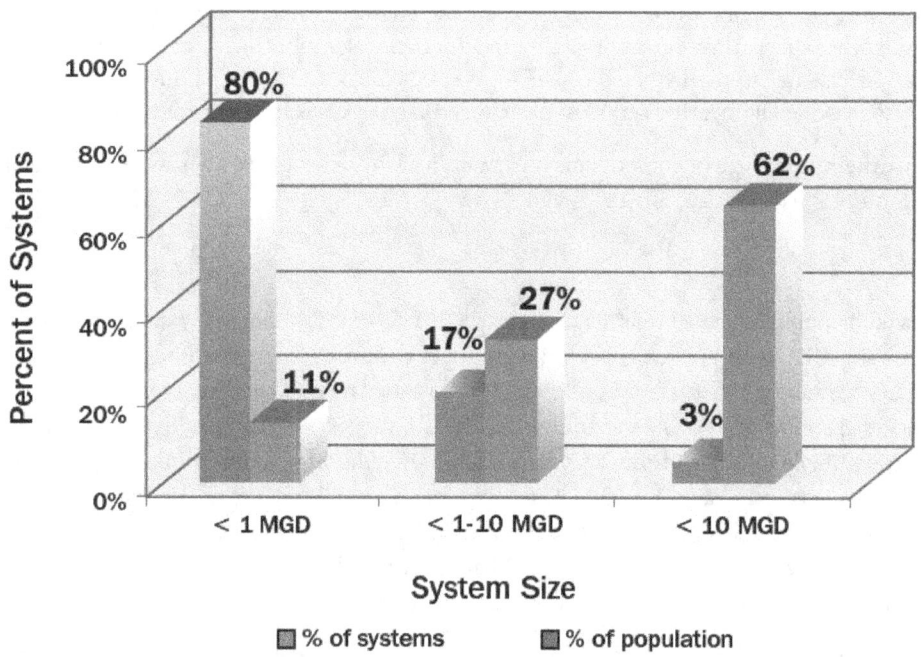

Wastewater utilities, also referred to as assets, contain several components, as listed below. These are divided into physical, cyber, and human elements.

Physical

• **Collection.** A network of pipes that conveys wastewater from the source to the treatment plant. In some older cities, the wastewater and stormwater collection systems are integrated in "combined sewer systems," and in wet weather the combined effluent may be discharged directly to the receiving body, bypassing the treatment plant.

• **Raw influent storage.** Raw sewage and industrial effluent stored in tanks or impoundments, generally for the purposes of flow equalization prior to treatment.

- **Treatment.** A variety of physical, biological, and chemical treatment processes applied to plant influent to reduce pollutant levels to concentrations specified in the NPDES permit, in the case of a direct discharger, or other specified discharge limits in the case of an indirect discharger.

- **Treated wastewater storage.** Treated wastewater held in lagoons prior to discharge.

- **Effluent/discharge.** The treated wastewater released to a surface water body, in the case of a direct discharger, or to a POTW collection system in the case of an indirect discharger.

- **Monitoring system.** Sensors installed at critical points to monitor a range of physical properties, such as flow rates and water quality indicators, and to detect levels of contaminants before, during, and after treatment.

Cyber

- **SCADA.** An electronic network, often including wireless communication that links the monitoring system and controls for the collection, treatment, and discharge systems to a central display and operations room. The system may include automated operation of controls based on the monitoring system readouts. A SCADA system may also help to automate control of a wastewater utility, with monitoring system readouts serving as inputs for control. The systems are part of an integrated control system essential to operation of a wastewater utility.

Human

- **Employees and contractors.** Wastewater utilities rely on part-time, full-time, and contract employees to manage and operate their facilities. Larger utilities also may have chemists, engineers, microbiologists, public relations people, security personnel, and other specialists who are highly trained in their roles individually and as a team. The training and availability of operators typically is based on the type, size, and complexity of the utility. Wastewater utilities also rely on cadres of outside contractors to provide engineering services, laboratory analyses, chemical deliveries, and security services.

Wastewater utilities differ in the type of components each has, and some may not have all the components listed above (e.g., small wastewater utilities may not have SCADA systems).

1.1.3 Key Authorities

A number of governing authorities pertain to the Water Sector. Most provide broad environmental authority that may support security-related activities and initiatives; some specifically address homeland security. Existing authorities provide for public health and environmental protection measures; identify and regulate hazardous chemical, radiological, and biological substances; provide for worker safety; ensure that the public receives information about water quality and chemical hazards; and provide enforcement authorities for EPA and State primacy agencies and permitting authorities that implement many of EPA's environmental laws. New security-related directives and authorities address collection of asset-specific information, further promote information sharing and protection, require vulnerability assessments and development of ERPs for certain sizes of CWSs, and encourage or require identification of protective strategies and implementation of protective programs.

Unless otherwise noted, the authorities identified below apply to drinking water and wastewater utilities (assets). A more detailed description of these and other authorities can be found in the Environmental Law Institute document *Homeland Security and Drinking Water-An Opportunity for Comprehensive Protection of a Vital Natural Resource*, published in October 2003. The following section breaks out pertinent authorities in several broad categories: (1) presidential directives; (2) general homeland security laws; and (3) drinking water and wastewater environmental laws. Other environmental laws that may affect the Water Sector and laws that apply to information access are summarized in appendix 2.

In May 1998, PDD-63 was signed. This directive set the administration's policy on critical infrastructure protection (CIP), identified key sectors, and assigned lead agencies for sector liaison. EPA was designated the lead for the Water Sector, working in cooperation with other Federal agencies and the public and private sectors. The directives described below are the most recent in a series of homeland security-related executive orders and presidential directives signed after PDD-63, and have the most impact on the Water Sector. They apply only to Federal agencies and do not impose any requirements on stakeholders.

1.1.3.1 Homeland Security Presidential Directive 7 (critical infrastructure identification, prioritization, and protection, December 17, 2003)

HSPD-7 establishes a national policy for Federal departments and agencies to identify and prioritize National CI/KR to protect them from terrorist attacks that could:

- Cause catastrophic health effects or mass casualties comparable to weapons of mass destruction (WMD);

- Impair the ability of Federal departments and agencies to perform essential missions or ensure protection of public health and safety;

- Undermine State and local government capacities to maintain order and deliver minimum essential public services;

- Damage the Water Sector's capability to ensure the orderly functioning of the economy and delivery of essential services;

- Have a negative impact on the economy through the cascading disruption of other CI/KR; and

- Undermine public morale and confidence in our national economic and political institutions.

The Secretary of Homeland Security is tasked with integrating and coordinating implementation efforts among Federal departments and agencies, State and local governments, and the Water Sector. The Secretary is to establish uniform policies, approaches, guidelines, and methodologies for integrating CIP and risk management activities within and across sectors, and for developing metrics as part of a national CI/KR protection plan. The Secretary also maintains an organization to serve as a focal point for cyber security, and prepares an annual Federal R&D plan to support this directive. Federal agencies are required to work with State and local governments and the Water Sector to accomplish these objectives, and are instructed to appropriately protect information associated with carrying out this directive. The directive focuses on CI/KR that, if exploited, could cause catastrophic health impacts or mass casualties and identifies EPA as the SSA for the Water Sector, known as the Drinking Water and Water Treatment Sector in this directive. HSPD-7 calls on SSAs to:

- Collaborate with Federal departments and agencies, State and local governments, and the Water Sector, and conduct or facilitate vulnerability assessments of the sector;

- Encourage risk management strategies to protect against and mitigate the effects of an attack; and

- Promote continued development of information-sharing and analysis mechanisms, in collaboration with the Water Sector.

1.1.3.2 Homeland Security Presidential Directive 8 (national preparedness-December 17, 2003)

HSPD-8 establishes policies to strengthen U.S. ability to prevent and respond to threatened or actual domestic terrorist attacks, major disasters, and other emergencies through development of a national, domestic all-hazards preparedness goal. It provides for State grants to build-through planning, training, and exercises-the capacity of first-responders to react to terrorist events. Funds also can be used to purchase equipment. States are required to develop state-specific plans. The directive also calls for development of quantifiable performance measures.

1.1.3.3 Homeland Security Presidential Directive 9 (defense of United States agriculture and food, January 30, 2004)

HSPD-9 establishes a national policy to defend the water, agriculture, and food system against terrorist attacks, major disasters, and other emergencies. It calls on EPA and other Federal agencies to:

- Build upon and expand current monitoring and surveillance programs for public health and water quality that provide early detection and awareness of disease, pest, or poisonous agents;

- Develop nationwide laboratory networks for water quality that integrate existing Federal and State laboratory resources;

- Develop and enhance intelligence capabilities to include collection and analysis of information concerning threats, delivery systems, and methods that could be directed against the Water Sector; and

- Accelerate and expand countermeasure research and development of detection methods, prevention technologies, agent characterization, and dose-response relationships for high-consequence agents.

1.1.3.4 Homeland Security Presidential Directive 10 (biodefense for the 21st century, April 24, 2004)

HSPD-10 provides a comprehensive framework for the Nation's biodefense. It builds on past accomplishments, specifies roles and responsibilities, and integrates the work of various communities-national security, medical, public health, intelligence, diplomatic, agricultural, and law enforcement-into a sustained and focused national effort against biological weapons threats. The directive focuses on threat awareness, prevention and protection, surveillance and detection, and response and recovery. Specific direction to departments and agencies to carry out this biodefense program is contained in a classified document.

Also included in this category is the Public Health Security and Bioterrorism Preparedness and Response Act of 2002 (Bioterrorism Act), but, because it explicitly amends the SDWA, the Act is discussed in conjunction with the SDWA information below.

The Water Sector is also governed by numerous environmental laws that regulate drinking water and wastewater utilities. The discussion below relates to EPA. Important to note, however, is that State governments most often have direct jurisdiction over drinking water and wastewater utilities, and they are most involved in fostering security at the local level through primacy agencies and permitting authorities. To obtain primacy, States and tribes must adopt regulations for contaminants that are no less stringent than EPA's regulations.

The following laws govern regulation of drinking water and wastewater utilities.

1.1.3.5 Safe Drinking Water Act, 42 United States Code (U.S.C.) 300F-300J-26

The general provisions of the SDWA, established in 1974, provide a basis for drinking water security by protecting water quality and underground sources of drinking water. To protect the quality of public drinking water, EPA established regulations for national primary and secondary drinking water standards. Forty-nine of the 50 States have received primacy from EPA to administer the drinking water program. To obtain primacy, States must adopt regulations no less stringent than the Federal Government's and must meet other conditions, described in more detail in appendix 2. Pertinent conditions include enforcement authority; the ability to conduct sanitary survey inspections of water utilities; and requirements to certify and approve laboratories for sample analysis, maintain an inventory of public water systems (utilities) in the State, and have an adequate plan to provide for safe drinking water during emergencies.

The statute applies to public water systems-systems for provision of water to the public for human consumption through pipes and other constructed conveyances, including such Federal facilities as military bases and hospitals, and other sites with their own drinking water systems. Drinking water programs most applicable to water security include wellhead protection and source water protection, protection of underground sources of drinking water, sanitary survey inspections, maintenance of records, and water quality monitoring.

1.1.3.6 Public Health Security and Bioterrorism Preparedness and Response Act of 2002, Public Law 107-188

Among other provisions, the Bioterrorism Act amends the SDWA by inserting Title IV, Drinking Water Security and Safety, into title XIV of the Public Health Services Act as sections 1433, 1434, and 1435. Initiatives and accomplishments under the act are as follows.

- In 2002, EPA provided the baseline probable threat information required to complete vulnerability assessments.

- On or before December 31, 2004, each CWS serving more than 3,300 persons conducted a vulnerability assessment, certified its completion, and submitted a copy to EPA.

- Each CWS serving more than 3,300 persons prepared or revised an ERP that incorporated the vulnerability assessment findings, and certified to EPA that the system had completed such a plan within 6 months of completing an assessment.

- EPA developed a protocol to protect this information.

- In June 2002, EPA developed vulnerability assessment guidance for systems serving 3,300 or fewer persons.

- EPA conducted research studies in:

  - Prevention, detection, and response to intentional introduction of contaminants into CWSs and their source water;

  - Methods and means by which terrorists could disrupt the supply of safe drinking water or act against drinking water infrastructure; and

  - Methods and means by which alternative supplies of drinking water could be provided in the event of destruction, impairment, or contamination of PWSs.

Important to note is that "vulnerability assessment" is the accepted terminology in the Water Sector due to the language of the Bioterrorism Act. The term is equivalent to the DHS's "risk assessment" since the methodologies developed for the Water Sector consider all the components of risk (consequence, threat, and vulnerability).

EPA has supported development of a suite of vulnerability (risk) assessment tools for drinking water and wastewater utilities of all sizes that address unique and fundamental security vulnerability concerns. All assessments were conducted at the utility level. Identification of priority components of a utility was dictated by local conditions, and determination of threats was made by the specific Water Sector utility conducting the assessment. As part of the vulnerability assessment, utilities develop inventories of system components, including physical, cyber, information technology (IT), and personnel components, and identify which components are most critical to the system's mission.

1.1.3.7 Federal Water Pollution Control Act (Clean Water Act), 33 U.S.C. 1251-1387

The CWA governs the quality of discharges to surface and groundwater. It establishes national, technology-based standards for municipal waste treatment and numerous categories of industrial point-source discharges (discharges from such fixed sources as pipes and ditches); requires States, and in some cases tribes, to enact and implement water quality standards to attain designated water-body uses; addresses water pollutants; and regulates dredge-and-fill activities and wetlands. The Act provides a number of enforcement authorities for EPA and States that have accepted permitting authority. It also applies these requirements to such Federal facilities as military installations and Department of Energy (DOE) sites. Provisions most applicable to security include the prohibition of discharges into waters of the United States, development of pretreatment effluent standards, oil and hazardous substance liability, and imminent and substantial endangerment authorities.

1.2 Security Partners

As described in section 1.1, the Water Sector, which includes drinking water and wastewater utilities, is well characterized and defined. EPA has a longstanding tradition of working through its 10 regional offices and with the 50 States, District of Columbia, tribes, and 6 Territories on oversight and implementation of regulations pertaining to the sector. Over time, EPA has developed relationships with local drinking water and wastewater utilities, directly and through the national organizations that represent their issues and concerns. The Agency uses many communication vehicles and mechanisms to solicit input from Water Sector entities and communicate regularly with them on a broad range of issues.

EPA historically has interacted with numerous Federal agencies in its mission to protect public health and the environment. These interactions have been expanded to include new Federal agencies that play roles in source water, drinking water, and wastewater security. Some of these agencies have been identified as having critical dependencies and interdependencies with the Water Sector, and efforts are underway to develop communication mechanisms to share information and improve the working relationships between the sectors at the national level. The relationships with these agencies and organizations are described more fully below.

1.2.1 Relationships With Sector-Specific Agencies

EPA works with the DHS to implement the National Infrastructure Protection Plan (NIPP) sector partnership model and risk management framework, develop protective programs and related requirements, and provide sector-level CI/KR protection guidance in line with overarching guidance established by the DHS under HSPD-7. EPA also provides sector performance feedback to the DHS to enable cross-sector CI/KR protection gap assessments. The Agency also encourages development of appropriate information-sharing and analysis mechanisms within the Water Sector.

The sector shares dependencies and interdependencies with other SSAs, including DOE, U.S. Department of Agriculture, Department of Health and Human Services, Department of Transportation, Department of the Interior, Department of Defense, and Department of State. EPA is responsible for working with these sectors to better identify, define, and address these interdependencies and vulnerabilities. These relationships are described in more detail below.

EPA relationship with the U.S. Department of Agriculture (USDA). EPA has a number of relationships with USDA. Historically it has worked closely with USDA's Rural Utilities Service, which provides funding and support for rural America, including small, rural drinking water and wastewater utilities. USDA's Forest Service works with EPA on source-water protection initiatives concerning sources of drinking water that lie or originate on Forest Service lands. The service also operates water utilities (at campgrounds, picnic grounds, and some ranger stations), and there are some community water system sources on National Forest land. With issuance of HSPD-9, EPA expanded its role with the USDA, as well as other Federal agencies, to build upon and expand current monitoring and surveillance programs that provide early detection and awareness of disease, pest, and poisonous agents.

EPA relationship with the Department of Health and Human Services (HHS). EPA has worked closely with several agencies within HHS, including the Centers for Disease Control and Prevention (CDC), Food and Drug Administration (FDA), and Indian Health Service. CDC and FDA in particular played important roles in helping EPA define biological, chemical, and radiological threats to drinking water. EPA has entered into a memorandum of agreement with CDC to leverage resources in the Laboratory Response Network (LRN), which includes private, State, and government laboratories and can mobilize quickly to test for possible terror-related contaminants. The agreement acknowledges that significant national laboratory testing capacity derives from use of established laboratory networks such as the LRN, Food Emergency Response Network (FERN), National Animal Health Laboratory Network, National Plant Diagnostic Network (NPDN), and Federal agencies with responsibility and authority for laboratory preparedness and response (collectively referred to as the Networks). The agreement respects existing relationships, policies, and operating procedures of the Networks or any similar group of laboratories with relationships involving Federal funding, direction, or other cooperative arrangements.

Furthermore, CDC counterparts are members of EPA's NHSRC Distribution System Research Consortium (DSRC), and FDA regulates bottled drinking water, which may be used as a short-term remedy when PWS service is interrupted. FDA is required to regulate bottled water to standards at least as stringent as those issued by EPA under the SDWA. The Water Sector also shares interdependencies with HHS regarding interstate conveyance carriers (e.g., planes and trains with potable water on board). EPA has a memorandum of understanding with FDA to deal with these carriers. Finally, as required under HSPD-9, EPA, with assistance from CDC and other Federal agencies, is implementing a pilot contaminant warning system for drinking water utilities.

EPA relationship with the Department of Energy (DOE). EPA has a number of relationships and dependencies/interdependencies with DOE. The primary interdependency is the need for a stable and reliable source of energy to power water and wastewater utilities. EPA also works closely with several DOE national laboratories, including Argonne, Lawrence Livermore, Los Alamos, and Sandia. These laboratories are represented on EPA's DSRC. The Agency worked with the Sandia lab, along with the American Water Works Association Research Foundation (AwwaRF), to develop a drinking water risk assessment tool that is used primarily by large drinking water systems to evaluate their threat vulnerabilities and consequences. The products of these efforts are tools and guidance for drinking water and wastewater utilities to minimize the likelihood that critical services will be disrupted as a result of cascading and escalating effects of either manmade or natural events.

EPA relationship with the Department of Transportation (DOT). DOT is responsible for promoting the safety, efficiency, effectiveness, and economic well-being of the Nation's transportation systems. The Water Sector shares several key interdependencies with DOT, including its reliance on the transportation sector to provide chemicals, such as gaseous chlorine, and supplies for drinking water and wastewater treatment facilities. Highways and railways can also present vulnerabilities to the Water Sector where they pass near or over sources of drinking water.

EPA relationship with the Department of the Interior (DOI). DOI's 824 dams and reservoirs provide water to 31 million people. EPA historically has worked with a number of Interior bureaus, including the National Park Service (NPS), U.S. Bureau of Reclamation (BuRec), Bureau of Land Management (BLM) U.S. Fish and Wildlife Service, and U.S. Geological Survey (USGS). USGS serves the Nation as a science agency that collects, monitors, analyzes, and provides scientific understanding of natural resources.

As part of its mission, USGS monitors and assesses the quality of source water, whether groundwater or surface water, providing data over long time scales with local, regional, national, and international perspectives. This USGS network could serve as the basis for field testing and developing chemical and biological weapon sensors, as well as collecting data on other potentially harmful water constituents.

In addition, USGS's National Water Quality Assessment program already provides periodic assessments that include data for many potentially harmful drinking water contaminants. In part, USGS's monitoring and research programs support EPA's regulatory and research agenda. EPA Region 2, USGS, and Rutgers University established a water security consortium in northern New Jersey to field test and deploy new water quality sensing technology for early-warning monitoring of hazards to water supplies. NPS maintains water and wastewater systems that are regulated by the SDWA and CWA. Several drinking water systems use BuRec dams, reservoirs, pumping plants, canals, and pipelines to provide drinking water. In addition, some water utility sources may lie on public lands managed by BLM. BLM also operates a number of TNCWSs (i.e. campgrounds) and plays a large role in managing and protecting the western water supply. The Tennessee Valley Authority plays a similarly important role for the southeastern water supply.

EPA relationship with the Department of Defense (DoD). The Agency's primary interaction with DoD is coordination with the U.S. Army Corps of Engineers (USACE), which is responsible for maintaining the Nation's commercial waterways and operates the dams and locks that facilitate commerce on inland waterways. A number of drinking water systems use dammed reservoirs as their primary water sources. Dam safety and protection is a critical issue for the Water Sector; some employees of the USACE Engineering Research and Development Center also sit on the EPA/NHSRC DSRC. Military facilities with their own drinking water and wastewater systems are regulated under the SDWA and CWA, and, where applicable, must complete and submit vulnerability assessments to EPA. USACE owns and operates the Washington Aqueduct, which supplies drinking water to the National Capital Area. EPA shares interdependencies with DoD. It works with DoD's Office of Naval Research, has developed an interagency agreement between DoD and NHSRC, and works with USACE to provide alternate water sources.

EPA relationship with the Department of State (DOS). It is critical for EPA to communicate and coordinate with the State Department to ensure that water quality and quantity issues are fully understood, and that steps are taken by our neighbors to the north and the south to protect water sources from potential terrorist attacks. Several major rivers used as sources of drinking water in the United States cross U.S. borders. In addition, a number of water utilities in the Northwest obtain their treatment chemicals from Canada. In its mission to create a more secure, democratic, and prosperous world, DOS collaborates with countries, government agencies, nongovernmental organizations, institutions of higher learning, and private sector partners. For example, it has helped EPA make proper contacts with Canada and Mexico to engage in revisions of the SSP and continue a dialogue to better protect national critical infrastructure.

1.2.2 Relationships With Public/Private Sector Owner/Operators, Technical Assistance, and Information Organizations

EPA most often communicates with the regional and national organizations that represent drinking water and wastewater utilities. These groups have regular communication with EPA through conference calls and meetings to discuss security projects and initiatives underway by the Agency and its sector security partners. EPA will continue to collaborate with these organizations on development and implementation of security strategies. The groups can call on their members to provide additional knowledge and technical expertise across the full range of CIP activities and issues. These organizations include:

Drinking Water and Wastewater

- **National Environmental Training Center for Small Communities.** The group helps small communities with populations up to 10,000 by providing training, related information, and referral services in wastewater, drinking water, and solid waste.

- **National Rural Water Association (NRWA).** The group represents 25,735 small and medium-size water utilities. NRWA's mission is to support its state rural-water associations, which represent these water and wastewater utilities.

- **Rural Community Assistance Program.** The group assists water and wastewater utilities serving populations fewer than 10,000. Most activities are carried out in rural areas with populations fewer than 2,000, in minority communities, and in underserved rural areas with a high percentage of low-income individuals.

Drinking Water

- **American Water Works Association (AWWA).** AWWA represents water utilities of all sizes and ownership types. Its 60,000-plus members represent the full spectrum of the drinking water community, including treatment plant operators and managers, scientists, environmentalists, manufacturers, academics, engineers, and regulators. Membership includes 4,700 utilities that supply water to 180 million North Americans.

- **American Water Works Association Research Foundation (AwwaRF).** A member-supported international nonprofit organization, AwwaRF sponsors research to enable water utilities, public health agencies, and other professionals to provide affordable drinking water to consumers.

- **Association of Metropolitan Water Agencies (AMWA).** AMWA represents the largest publicly owned drinking water systems in the United States. Collectively, member agencies serve 120 million people. AMWA is the industry lead for the Water Sector and oversees the Water Information Sharing and Analysis Center (WaterISAC) and Water Security Channel (WaterSC). The WaterISAC is a centralized resource that gathers, analyzes, and disseminates threat information specific to the Water Sector. It serves drinking water and wastewater utilities of all sizes and ownership types, and is supported through subscriber fees and EPA grants. It has the most comprehensive and readily available online library that includes contaminant databases and resources about Water Sector vulnerabilities, incidents, and solutions for all hazards. The WaterSC is a supplementary service of the WaterISAC intended to reach a larger Water Sector audience. The WaterSC is an e-mail notification service and Web site that is a free and password-protected information portal for utilities. It sends e-mail alerts on security issues directly to more than 11,000 subscribers.

- **National Association of Water Companies (NAWC).** NAWC is the only national trade association exclusively representing all aspects of the private water service industry. The range of its members' business includes ownership of regulated drinking water and wastewater utilities, and the many forms of public/private partnerships and management contract arrangements. Its members provide drinking water to 22 million people across the country. NAWC members are regulated at the Federal level by EPA and at the State level by State health and environment agencies. Members are economically regulated by State public utility commissions.

- **State Operator Certification and Technical Assistance Program Trainers.** Under the 1996 SDWA amendments, EPA funds trainers and technical assistance providers through the Drinking Water State Revolving Loan Fund and Expense Reimbursement Grant Program.

Wastewater

- **National Association of Clean Water Agencies (NACWA).** NACWA represents the interests of more than 300 public agencies and organizations that serve the majority of the sewered population in the United States. Members collectively treat and reclaim more than 18 billion gallons of wastewater daily.

- **State On-Site Operator and Technical Assistance Program Trainers.** Authorized under CWA section 104(g) and partially funded by EPA, these trainers provide financial, technical, and operations and maintenance (O&M) assistance to small municipal wastewater treatment plants through direct on-site operator training.

- **Water Environment Federation (WEF).** WEF is composed of individual members and member associations representing engineers, public and private plant operators and managers, students, laboratory technicians, wastewater consultants, retired wastewater professionals, and public officials.

- **Water Environment Research Foundation (WERF).** WERF is dedicated to advancing science and technology that addresses water quality. Subscribers include individuals and organizations from municipal agencies, academia, government laboratories, and industrial and consulting firms.

1.2.3 Relationships With Department of Homeland Security

EPA continually communicates and coordinates with the DHS on Water Sector security. The Agency works with the DHS in implementing various presidential directives, executive orders, and statutes. To improve these efforts, EPA has selected one full-time employee within its Water Security Division to work directly with the DHS; this person is designated as the Water Sector liaison to the DHS. The liaison helps to coordinate and share information between DHS and EPA pertaining to water-sector security. EPA also has coordinated with the DHS's Office of Grants and Training (G&T) to provide emergency response training to drinking water systems serving more than 100,000 persons. EPA continues this effort for small and medium-size drinking water utilities and large wastewater utilities.

EPA's NHSRC coordinates regularly with the DHS Science and Technology (S&T) Directorate to exchange information on research needs, and to discuss priorities and gaps for the Water Sector in a wide range of security-related research areas. The NHSRC is engaged in S&T's CIP R&D Program; the first program meeting for sector-specific agencies was held in early 2005, and additional meetings are being planned. Once DHS's decision support system is complete, utilities might use the model to assess interdependencies. Department staffers are members of EPA's DSRC, and EPA works closely with the Federal Emergency Management Agency (FEMA) to address natural disasters and security issues as they relate to the Water Sector.

EPA coordinates with the DHS to receive timely water-related threat information (classified and unclassified) and information on the content and distribution of threat-warning products. EPA provides the DHS with an understanding of the vulnerability and consequence issues that directly impact Water Sector utilities. The Agency stands ready to coordinate with the DHS to provide additional information about threats to utilities.

1.2.4 Relationships With Other Federal Departments and Agencies

EPA relationship with Homeland Security Council (HSC). The President established the HSC to ensure coordination of all security-related activities among executive departments and agencies, and to promote effective development and implementation of all homeland security policies. The HSC is composed of the Principals Committee, Deputies Committee, and Policy Coordination Committee. EPA participates in committee meetings when issues pertaining to its responsibilities and expertise are discussed.

EPA relationship with Federal Energy Regulatory Commission (FERC). FERC is an independent agency that regulates interstate transmission of natural gas, oil, and electricity. It also regulates natural gas and hydropower projects, and oversees environmental matters related to these projects and major electricity policy initiatives. EPA's interaction with FERC primarily involves discussions of the Water Sector's interdependency with electric power.

EPA relationship with Federal Bureau of Investigation (FBI). EPA, the DHS, and the WaterISAC work closely with the FBI to share intelligence and threat warnings related to physical and cyber attacks and to contamination. The FBI and EPA prepare and update threat information related to drinking water and wastewater. Drinking water and wastewater utilities, as well as States, have been encouraged by EPA to coordinate security activities with local FBI offices nationwide. EPA has also developed tools and outreach documents to educate the law enforcement community about drinking water and wastewater utilities. It has offered Water Security Awareness training to the FBI's Joint Terrorism Task Force to provide an understanding of water systems, their vulnerabilities and current threats, and response measures.

EPA relationship with Federal Communications Commission (FCC). The FCC is an independent agency of the United States directly responsible to Congress. Established by the Communications Act of 1934, it is charged with regulating interstate and international communications by radio, television, wire, satellite, and cable. The FCC's jurisdiction covers the 50 States, District of Columbia, and U.S. possessions. The Water Sector shares interdependencies with the FCC vis-à-vis the vulnerabilities of communication transmission equipment located on drinking water towers.

EPA relationship with Central Intelligence Agency (CIA). The CIA coordinates the Nation's intelligence activities, and correlates, evaluates, and disseminates intelligence that affects national security. It also engages in research, development, and deployment of technology for intelligence purposes, and provides an independent source of analysis on national and international concerns. EPA works directly with the CIA to ensure the flow of intelligence in support of homeland defense related to the Water Sector.

1.2.5 Relationships With State and Local Governments

As noted previously, EPA depends heavily on State drinking water primacy agencies and the wastewater permitting authorities that implement the SDWA and CWA. Because almost all drinking water and most wastewater programs are delegated to the States, EPA must work with them to ensure implementation of programmatic and security-related initiatives. In addition to Federal programmatic responsibilities, States also have their own initiatives and priorities. The State programs maintain inventories of drinking water and wastewater facilities, regularly inspect these utilities, provide technical assistance, maintain laboratory and operator certification programs, and monitor compliance by reviewing analytical results. States review and approve plans and specifications for new and expanded drinking water and wastewater facilities, and take enforcement actions as needed.

Because of the primacy and permitting relationship with the States, EPA works very closely with the two organizations that represent State drinking water and wastewater programs:

- The Association of State Drinking Water Administrators (ASDWA) represents drinking water agencies in the States, District of Columbia, Territories, commonwealths, and tribes of the United States; and

- The Association of State and Interstate Water Pollution Control Administrators (ASIWPCA) represents wastewater programs in the same jurisdictions.

EPA is coordinating its security efforts and initiatives with these State and local entities that represent the Water Sector. This coordination includes facilitating meetings, seeking input on sector security concerns and issues, and raising security awareness. Many of these entities are used as conduits to get information and training opportunities to utilities.

EPA communicates with these associations regularly and meets frequently with State workgroups to discuss issues and set priorities. The Agency also meets with association members at their annual conferences, meetings, and special events such as security workshops. EPA regional offices frequently communicate with State programs.

The Agency also works through various other national organizations that represent these constituencies and related services and interests. These organizations include the:

• American Public Works Association, a 26,000-member international educational and professional association of public agencies, private sector companies, and individuals dedicated to providing high-quality public works goods and services;

• Association of Public Health Laboratories (APHL), which represents the Nation's public health and environmental laboratories. In an effort to strengthen the Nation's laboratory capability and capacity, EPA and APHL have formed a partnership to formulate sound public health and environmental policies, offer training and education, and improve overall laboratory management and practices nationwide;

• Association of State and Territorial Health Officials, which represents public health agencies of the States, Territories, and District of Columbia;

• Environmental Council of the States, which represents State and territorial environmental commissioners;

• International City/County Management Association, a professional and educational organization composed of 8,000 chief appointed managers, administrators, and assistants in cities, towns, counties, and regional entities in the United States and throughout the world;

• National Association of Counties, which represents the interests of 2,000 of the 3,066 counties across the United States that cover 80 percent of the Nation's population;

• National Association of County and City Health Officials, which represents local public health agencies, including city, county, metropolitan, district, and tribal agencies;

• National Conference of State Legislatures, a bipartisan organization that serves the legislators and staffs of the States and Territories;

• National Governors Association, which represents the Nation's governors;

• National League of Cities, which works with 49 State municipal leagues to represent 18,000 State league cities and 1,700 member cities;

• State Homeland Security Advisors, a network of contacts that the Governor of each State has appointed to coordinate homeland security activities; and

• U.S. Conference of Mayors, a nonpartisan organization of the 1,183 U.S. cities with populations greater than 30,000.

Through this extensive network, EPA can communicate quickly and efficiently with State and local governments. The broad perspectives and extensive memberships of many of these organizations allow feedback and input on interdependencies, and provide a basis for establishing security priorities in the Water Sector that complement actions taken at the local level. EPA communicates with these organizations through conference calls and meetings, and solicits their input on security policy decisions.

1.2.6 Relationships With Tribal Governments

Tribal governments are treated similar to the State and local partners in the Water Sector. EPA provides security-related outreach to tribes primarily through its regional offices. The tribes receive the same information and have access to the same tools and products that EPA has developed for the entire Water Sector.

1.2.7 Relationships With Advisory Councils

Protecting the Nation's CI/KR requires partnerships among Federal, State, territorial, tribal, and local governments and private sector infrastructure owner/operators, both within and across sectors. The goal of these partnerships is to establish the context, framework, and support for coordination and information-sharing activities required to implement a full spectrum of prudent and responsible protective actions. EPA coordinates its security efforts with a number of advisory councils, such as the WSCC and GCC, to seek input, direction, and to identify gaps and next steps on a wide range of CIP activities.

In September 2004, the WSCC was formed by eight drinking water and wastewater organizations (AWWA, AwwaRF, AMWA, NACWA, NAWC, NRWA, WEF, and WERF). The WSCC is composed of water utility managers appointed by the associations and members of each of the associations. The founding associations developed the WSCC's mission: "The Water Sector Coordinating Council shall serve as a policy, strategy, and coordination mechanism and recommend actions to reduce and eliminate significant homeland security vulnerabilities to the Water Sector through interaction with the Federal government and other critical infrastructure sectors." WSCC members play a critical liaison role between the WSCC, GCC, and broader Water Sector community across the full range of infrastructure protection activities and issues within the parameters of the NIPP sector partnership model and as supported by the Critical Infrastructure Partnership Advisory Council (CIPAC).

The Water Sector GCC enables interagency and cross-jurisdictional coordination. It is composed of representatives from various levels of government-Federal, State, territorial, tribal, and local. The GCC was formed in January 2005 and meets as needed. Members include representatives of EPA, DHS (FEMA), DoD (USACE), DOI (BuRec), FERC, DOS, HHS (CDC and the Office of Public Health Emergency Preparedness), USDA, ASDWA, and ASIWPCA. The Water Sector's GCC coordinates strategies, activities, policies, and communication across government entities. The WSCC and GCC work together to coordinate sector CIP activities.

1.2.8 Relationships With Academia, Research Centers, and Think Tanks

EPA has established working relationships with a number of research organizations such as the AwwaRF, WERF, and Sandia and Argonne national laboratories. These entities and others conduct research, identify gaps, and develop security-related tools and products. The academic and research center communities play important roles in enabling national CI/KR protection and implementation of the NIPP, including:

- Supporting research, development, testing, evaluation, and deployment of CIP technologies;

- Analyzing, developing, and sharing best practices related to CIP efforts;

- Preparing or disseminating guidelines, courses, and descriptions of best practices for physical and cyber security;

- Developing and providing suitable security risk analysis and risk management courses for CIP professionals; and

- Conducting research to identify new technologies and analytical methods that can be applied by security partners to support CIP efforts.

Many of these activities could help to secure the Water Sector. EPA will continue to work with other Water Sector security partners to determine if and how academia, research centers, and think tanks can help enhance the sector's security posture.

1.2.9 Relationships With International Organizations and Foreign Countries

In the aftermath of the September 11 attacks, the U.S., Canadian, and Mexican governments have focused a great deal of attention on their shared borders. Recognizing the need to protect their citizens and critical infrastructure from terrorist attack, the United States and Canada signed the Smart Border Declaration in December 2001. The declaration, which includes a 30-point action plan, has as a goal promoting legitimate travel and commerce across the U.S.-Canada border while protecting both countries from crime and terrorism. A similar accord was signed with Mexico in March 2002, accompanied by a 22-point action plan that outlined specific actions to determine and address security risks while efficiently and effectively expediting the flow of legitimate goods and people across the U.S.-Mexico border.

In November 2002, the United States and Mexico developed the Critical Infrastructure Protection Framework Agreement. The U.S.-Mexico Action Plan provided that the countries would conduct bi-national vulnerability assessments of trans-border infrastructure and communications and transportation networks to identify problems and take protective action. The CIP Agreement provides a cooperative framework under which bi-national guidelines are to be developed for CIP in seven sectors under the general direction of the DHS. Working groups were developed for each sector (Energy, Transportation, Communications, Water/Dams and Public Health/Agriculture) and lead U.S. and Mexican agencies were identified to co-chair each group.

The International Boundary and Water Commission co-chairs the Water/Dams Working Group established under the 2002 CIP Agreement and takes a lead role in implementing the Sector Protection Plan's critical infrastructure goal. The commission has formed a bi-national task force that includes representatives of other relevant U.S. and Mexican water-related agencies. The task force has inventoried and charted shared and non-shared critical infrastructure along the Rio Grande, Colorado, and Tijuana rivers. The working group has identified and implemented preliminary security upgrades as a short-term action. It intends to conduct more comprehensive bi-national vulnerability assessments of each infrastructure component identified as critical, and to adopt detection, delay, or response mitigation measures to enhance security, subject to available funding.

On July 19, 2005, EPA signed a Statement of Intent with the Ministry of National Infrastructures of Israel to assist with CIP activities. The Statement of Intent helps to foster collaboration; assists with identifying expertise from relevant sectors; encourages the exchange of experiences; identifies gaps in shared knowledge; and works to exchange information on chemical, biological, and radiological threats, the research and development of monitoring and warning systems, real-time emergency response, and research in the areas of risk assessment and risk management.

In July 2005, EPA hosted a CIP meeting with the United Kingdom Drinking Water Inspectorate that has led to technical exchanges on emergency response, contaminant information, sampling and analysis for unknown contaminants, backflow prevention, decontamination, risk communication, and program design and evaluation. Informal dialogue has also been initiated with the Netherlands, Australia, and the Czech Republic. EPA is establishing contacts with Mexico and Canada to develop a more formal water security relationship. More information on international coordination can be found in section 8 of the SSP.

1.3 Sector Security Goals

Sector security goals state the comprehensive protective posture that the government and infrastructure owners and operators are working together to achieve. As identified in the NIPP, critical infrastructure protection security goals should reflect the overall risk management outcomes that owners/operators and government leaders seek to produce for their sectors. Furthermore, the desired protective posture in each sector should be built using the full spectrum of protective activities-prevention, detection, response to, and recovery from terrorist attacks, other intentional acts, natural disasters, and other hazards as defined in the risk management framework of the NIPP.

Through a collaborative process, EPA and a joint working group of the WSCC and GCC have developed a security vision statement and a suite of security goals that provide clear direction for the Water Sector's CI/KR protection efforts. The sector's vision is as follows:

1.3.1 Elements and Characteristics of Sector Security Goals

EPA's Water Sector security mission statement aligns directly with the risk management framework outlined in the NIPP. The sector's vision statement supports this framework and is the foundation for its security goals. The subsequent elements of these vision and mission statements increase in specificity as the risk management framework is applied to identify the specific activities necessary to achieve the desired protective posture of the sector. Figure 1-4 illustrates how the mission and vision statements support development of security goals, objectives, and milestones, ultimately leading to measurement of security progress. These elements will be used by the sector to develop and implement protective programs and measure progress as discussed in subsequent sections of the SSP.

Figure 1-4: Sector Strategic Planning Framework

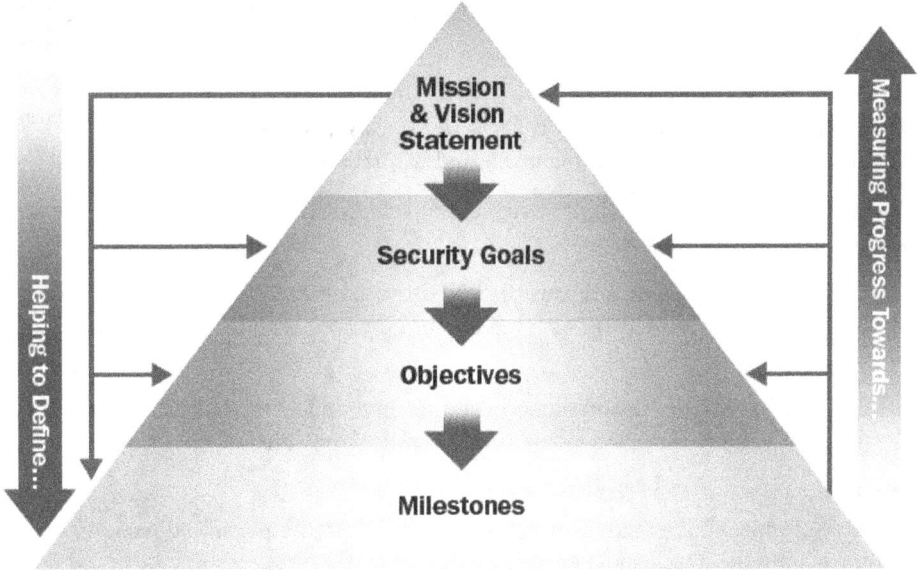

Protective actions are activities designed to prevent, detect, respond to, and recover from terrorist attacks, other intentional acts, natural disasters, and other hazards (the all-hazards approach). These actions reduce vulnerability to attack or other disaster, minimize consequences, and enable timely, efficient response and restoration following an event. Based on the Water Sector's security vision statement, four overarching strategic goals have been enumerated:

1. Sustain protection of public health and the environment;

2. Recognize and reduce risks in the Water Sector;

3. Maintain a resilient infrastructure; and

4. Increase communication, outreach, and public confidence.

The WSCC and GCC have collaborated with EPA to identify a list of objectives that support each goal. These goals and objectives focus on the concepts of prevention, detection, response, and recovery. They also satisfy the sector's vision and the NIPP framework, and they guide EPA's strategic planning process for sector security. The goals and objectives are at various stages of planning and implementation.

Goal 1: Sustain protection of public health and the environment. The Nation relies on a sustained amount of safe drinking water and on treatment of wastewater to maintain public health and environmental protection. To help better protect and secure public and environmental health, the Water Sector will work to ensure the continuity of both drinking water and wastewater services.

• **Objective 1:** Encourage integration of security concepts into daily business operations at utilities to foster a security culture.

• **Objective 2:** Evaluate and develop security-related surveillance, monitoring, warning, and response capabilities to recognize risks introduced into Water Sector systems that affect public health and economic viability.

• **Objective 3:** Develop a nationwide laboratory network for water quality security that integrates Federal and State laboratory resources and uses standardized diagnostic protocols and procedures, or develop a supporting laboratory network capable of analyzing security threats to water quality.

Goal 2: Recognize and reduce risks in the Water Sector. With an improved understanding of the vulnerabilities, threats, and consequences, owner/operators of utilities can continue to thoroughly examine and implement risk-based approaches to better protect, detect, respond to, and recover from manmade and natural events.

• **Objective 1:** Improve identification of vulnerabilities based on knowledge and best available information, with the intent of increasing the sector's overall security posture.

• **Objective 2:** Improve identification of potential threats through sector partners' (water utilities; national associations; and Federal, State, and local governments) knowledge base and communications with the intent of increasing overall sector security posture.

• **Objective 3:** Identify and refine public health and economic impact consequences of manmade or natural incidents to improve utility risk assessments and enhance the sector's overall security posture.

Goal 3: Maintain a resilient infrastructure. The Water Sector will investigate how to optimize continuity of operations to ensure the economic vitality of communities and the utilities that serve them. Response and recovery from an incident in the sector will be crucial to maintaining public health and confidence.

• **Objective 1:** Emphasize continuity of drinking water and wastewater services as it pertains to utility emergency preparedness, response, and recovery planning.

• **Objective 2:** Explore and expand implementation of mutual aid agreements/compacts in the Water Sector. The sector has significantly enhanced its resilience through agreements among utilities and States; increasing the number and scope of these will further enhance resiliency.

• **Objective 3:** Identify and implement key response and recovery strategies. Response and recovery from an incident in the sector will be crucial to maintaining public health and confidence.

- **Objective 4:** Increase understanding of how the sector is interdependent with other critical infrastructure sectors. Sectors such as Public Health and Emergency Services are largely dependent on the Water Sector for their continuity of operations, while the Water Sector is dependent on sectors such as Chemical and Electricity for continuity of its operations.

Goal 4: Increase communication, outreach, and public confidence. Safe drinking water and water quality are fundamental to everyday life. An incident in the Water Sector could have significant impacts on public confidence. Fostering and enhancing the relationships between utilities, government, and the public can mitigate negative perceptions in the face of an incident.

- **Objective 1:** Communicate with the public about the level of security and resilience in the Water Sector and provide outreach to ensure the public's ability to be prepared and respond to a natural disaster or manmade incident.
- **Objective 2:** Enhance communication and coordination among utilities and Federal, State, and local officials and agencies to provide information about threats.
- **Objective 3:** Improve relationships among all Water Sector security partners through a strong public-private partnership characterized by trusted relationships.

These goals and objectives will help drive development and implementation of protective programs described in section 5 and measures of progress described in section 6 of the SSP.

1.3.2 Process to Establish Sector Security Goals

Under the DHS's CIPAC, EPA established a collaborative and interactive process for developing Water Sector goals that included involvement with the WSCC, GCC, DHS, and other sector security partners. Select members of the GCC and WSCC formed an SSP working group, and in collaboration with EPA created an SSP-completion timeline and development approach consisting of facilitated face-to-face meetings and conference calls. The GCC and WSCC provided strategic direction and guidance to EPA in developing the sections of the SSP prior to full sector review. EPA created a password-protected Web site that allowed access to SSP-related materials and draft sections of the SSP. This Web site was used as a portal for evaluation and allowed users to view comments on the SSP made by others. The process was open and iterative, allowed for multiple opportunities to provide input and recommendations, and assisted EPA in development and finalization of the Water SSP.

1.4 Value Proposition

Efficiently and effectively securing the physical, human, and cyber elements of the Water Sector necessitates significant contributions from all sector security partners. These contributions require time and energy and, in many circumstances, financial and other resources from the owner/ operators of CI/KR. While the expenses for governmental security partners are typically executively or legislatively mandated and funded through governmental appropriations, the non-Federal security partners for the most part do not receive such funding. However, as traditional stewards of public health and the environment, drinking water and wastewater utilities work to ensure continuity of operations to sustain protection of public health and the environment. This concept manifests itself in the Water Sector's security vision statement and its goals, and the need to be prepared for all hazards aligns with the sector's security culture.

Water Sector owner/operators and other security partners continue to enhance security of the Nation's critical water infrastructure. These activities have additional benefits, such as:

- The satisfaction of contributing to protection of the Nation, the American people, national economy, and American way of life;
- The ability to provide input to the design of Federal, State, and local security programs that may better protect and prepare utilities against all hazards;

- Influencing the allocation of Federal, State, and local funds and other resources that may help secure the Water Sector's infrastructure;

- Receipt of timely, accurate, and useful information on threats to the sector, as well as receipt of protective best practices/ assessment methodologies and other information and tools that can help utility owner/operators better assess and protect their assets and investments from all hazards;

- Improved relationships with EPA, the DHS, and other government agencies on security and emergency preparedness;

- Influencing the type of environment through which Water Sector security and emergency preparedness is promoted; and

- Enhanced cyber security postures that can prevent business interruption or loss or misuse of sensitive information.

These mutual benefits enhance Water Sector owner/operators' ability to prevent, detect, respond to, and recover from all hazards, including terrorist attacks and natural disasters. Integrating security and developing an all-hazards approach to asset protection increases preparedness and resiliency to better ensure continuity of services from utilities.

2. Identify Assets, Systems, Networks, and Functions

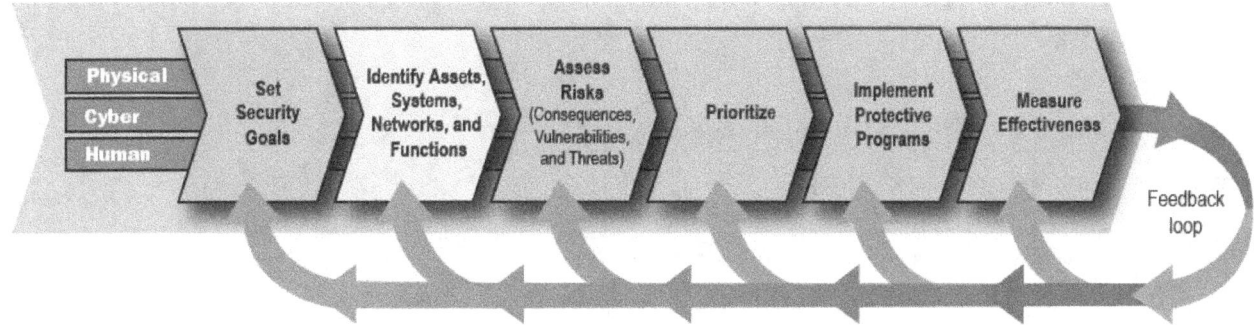

Continuous improvement to enhance protection of CI/KR

This section of the SSP discusses the ongoing efforts by government security partners and Water Sector public/private security partners to help identify assets that could, if compromised, result in significant economic damage or human casualties. Also discussed are relevant information parameters and data sources that are available to assist the Water Sector in conducting risk management activities and protecting infrastructure assets and systems.

2.1 Defining Information Parameters

Drinking water and wastewater assets are defined as entire utilities for purposes of identification, prioritization, and coordination in the Water Sector. Owners and operators are responsible for conducting risk assessments of their utilities to identify components (e.g., pumps, generators, SCADA systems) the loss or damage of which, due to manmade or natural events, could adversely affect the utility's operation, threaten public health or the environment, or have significant economic impacts. Critical Water Sector infrastructure is owned and operated predominantly by the public sector (i.e., local government). EPA, the DHS, and Water Sector owner/operators and security partners will continue to work together to develop more robust threat, vulnerability, and consequence information in order to assist water-sector utilities identify their most critical components.

The Water Sector is composed of a diverse set of drinking water and wastewater utilities. Characteristics of these utilities that are useful for defining sector infrastructure information are available in databases that EPA maintains (these are described more fully later in this section).

The following categories for drinking water and wastewater utilities are commonly used in the Water Sector and are captured in EPA's databases, and should be reflected in the NADB.

Drinking Water Utilities

- Utility type: CWS, TNCWS, NTNCWS;

- Population served (small, medium, large);

- Number of drinking water treatment plants;

- Source water: ground water, surface water, or ground water under the influence of surface water;

- Treatment type:

  – Disinfection method;

- Geographic location; and

- Chemicals stored on site.

Wastewater Utilities

- Population served;

- Sewer type: combined sewer overflow, sanitary sewer overflow;

- Treatment type (primary, secondary, tertiary):

  – Disinfection method;

- Geographic location; and

- Chemicals stored on site.

2.1.1 Collecting Infrastructure Information

SSAs are required to provide the best information possible to the DHS. In coordination with the Water Sector, EPA maintains several databases that contain general data on drinking water and wastewater utilities. These databases are important in describing and quantifying identifying information about the sector. However, as the DHS recognizes in its SSP guidance to SSAs, specific security information is generally held by owner/operators. If this information is needed, it will need to be submitted voluntarily. Submission of such information will require that all security partners work together to develop processes for collecting, protecting, and storing data that meet individual needs and address particular concerns.

Regarding asset identification, EPA does not anticipate the need to initiate data collection efforts beyond current levels. Large CIP-focused data collection efforts on the part of government agencies are not required because EPA already has the mechanisms in place to collect information on Water Sector assets. When appropriate and necessary, established communication channels will be used to communicate more detailed information among industry, government, and other sector security partners.

2.1.2 EPA Databases

EPA maintains several databases mandated by statute or regulation that contain relevant information about drinking water and wastewater utilities. As part of its mission under the SDWA and CWA, EPA maintains general information about its inventory of regulated entities. In response to requirements of these acts, EPA conducts surveys of Water Sector infrastructure (e.g., the Drinking Water Infrastructure Needs Survey and Assessment and the Clean Watersheds Needs Survey) for reports to Congress every four years. These reports are also available to the public. EPA receives information from States to maintain an inventory of drinking water and wastewater utilities for its databases, which are described below.

2.1.2.1 Drinking Water

Safe Drinking Water Information System (SDWIS). This database contains a complete inventory of all PWSs. Data relevant to security include system type, activity status, service population, water source, type of asset, detailed location information, treatment in place, and type of area served (e.g., residential, school, mobile home park). Utilities report data to the States, which collect and upload the information electronically every quarter to an EPA database (SDWIS/Fed). EPA Region 8 performs this function for Wyoming, which does not have primacy. This database was used as the primary source to characterize drinking water utilities, allocate resources and assistance, and track compliance with deadlines of the Bioterrorism Act.

Drinking Water Infrastructure Needs Survey. Data are collected from a survey of approximately 4,500 CWSs; this includes a census of all utilities serving populations of 40,000 or more and a statistical sample of those serving smaller populations. The survey has been updated every four years since 1995; the 2003 survey was published in 2005. Extensive data on needed upgrades, replacement, or construction of new assets are collected. Because the survey focuses on needs, however, it gives less than complete information on assets in place.

Community Water System Survey. The quadrennial survey is a national statistical sample intended to provide estimates of the operating and financial characteristics of CWSs by size category, water source, and ownership type. It is complete only for systems serving more than 100,000 persons. Information relevant to water security includes water exchanges with other systems, volumes drawn and stored, capacity and production of each treatment plant, treatment in place, use of a SCADA system, and length and age of distribution mains. Maps and other sensitive information are not available in the electronic database.

2.1.2.2 Wastewater

Permit Compliance System (PCS). PCS is a national database that contains information on POTWs and industrial dischargers. It is updated quarterly by the permitting authority. Information pertinent to security includes the average permitted flow, type of industrial activity that produces the waste stream (in the case of industrial dischargers), and details on the water body that receives the discharge. PCS is readily accessed by the public via the Internet.

Clean Watersheds Needs Survey. The survey represents only municipal dischargers permitted by NPDES; there is no comparable system for reporting infrastructure needs for industrial dischargers. The data are collected and entered into EPA's database by the permitting authority. This survey has been updated every four years since its inception and contains information on needed upgrades, replacements, and expansions of such assets as treatment plants and sewers. The survey also collects such design information as treatment plant capacity and length of sewer pipe.

2.1.3 National Asset Database

The DHS maintains and is enhancing a comprehensive catalog that includes an inventory and descriptive information about the assets and systems that make up the Nation's critical infrastructure. The NADB allows analysis of consequences, specific and common vulnerabilities, dependencies, and interdependencies within and across sectors and geographic regions.

To assist the DHS in developing the NADB, EPA provided from its existing databases the following information on Water Sector assets:

- Name of utility;
- Location of utility;
- Point-of-contact information (e.g., telephone number, e-mail address);
- Population served;
- Type of drinking water utility (e.g., year-round or seasonal);
- Source of drinking water (e.g., ground water, surface water);
- Type of wastewater effluent discharge (e.g., surface water, ground water);

- Treatment type (e.g., filtered, unfiltered);

- Wastewater treatment type (e.g., primary, secondary, tertiary);

- Longitude and latitude of treatment plant;

- Drinking water intake(s) or well locations;

- Wastewater effluent discharge location(s);

- Drinking water distribution system area;

- Wastewater collection system area; and

- Chemicals stored on site.

EPA has worked with the DHS to ensure that the NADB framework accurately reflects the Water Sector. Pursuant to a DHS data call to all SSAs in summer 2005, EPA provided a list of sector assets for its NADB built on the DHS's criteria of population served. It is working with the WSCC to improve the quality of these data using public health impact and economic disruption as criteria, and using consequence analysis, vulnerability data, and threat information for asset selection. A process to identify higher consequence assets in the Water Sector will be discussed in section 4 of this SSP.

2.1.4 Public Health Security and Bioterrorism Preparedness and Response Act of 2002

Under the Bioterrorism Act, each CWS serving more than 3,300 persons is required to conduct and submit a vulnerability (risk) assessment to EPA.

At a minimum, these assessments must include an evaluation of:

- Pipes and constructed conveyances;

- Physical barriers;

- Water collection, pretreatment, and treatment;

- Storage and distribution facilities;

- Electronic, computer, or other automated systems used by the CWS;

- Use, storage, or handling of various chemicals; and

- O&M of the system.

Furthermore, based on the findings of those risk assessments, these CWSs were also required to develop or update ERPs based on the findings of their assessment and certify completion of such actions to the Agency.

There is no requirement for other sizes or types of drinking water systems or for wastewater systems to conduct or submit risk assessments and ERPs. There is recognition, however, that a significant portion of drinking water and wastewater utilities not affected by the Bioterrorism Act have voluntarily taken steps to assess their risks and develop or update ERPs.

2.1.5 Risk Assessment Tools

As previously noted, all risk assessments are conducted at the asset level; identification of priority components at that level is dictated by local conditions. Threat information is provided by the Federal Government, and individual utilities apply that information during their risk assessments. Utilities use the findings of risk assessments to prioritize actions needed to prevent, detect, respond to, and recover from terrorist attacks, other intentional acts, natural disasters, and other hazards (all-hazards approach).

EPA has supported development of risk assessment tools for drinking water and wastewater systems of all sizes. These tools address unique and fundamental security concerns.

This suite of risk assessment tools supports the DHS's risk management framework and takes into consideration the criteria of its Risk Assessment Methodology for Critical Asset Protection (RAMCAP) as outlined in the NIPP. The criteria include:

- **Deterrence capabilities:** The ability to deter an attack by affecting the adversary's perception of its capability or the level of effort required to execute a successful attack;

- **Detection capabilities:** The ability to identify or expose an attack before it takes place;

- **Devaluing capabilities:** The ability to reduce an attacker's incentive to attack by reducing the value of the target;

- **Defensive (delay and denial) capabilities:** The ability to prevent an attack or delay it long enough for security or law enforcement personnel to mount an effective response;

- **Response capabilities:** The ability to effectively respond to an attack underway;

- **Consequence reduction/mitigation capabilities:** The ability to limit consequences should an attack occur; and

- **Recovery capabilities:** The ability to return to an acceptable level of operations after an attempted or successful attack.

As part of the risk assessment, utilities develop an inventory of asset components including physical, cyber, IT, and personnel, and they identify which components are most critical to their mission. Common to all of these risk assessment methodologies are these six elements:

- Characterization of the system, including its mission and objectives;

- Identification and prioritization of adverse consequences to avoid;

- Determination of critical assets that might be subject to malevolent acts that could result in undesired consequences;

- Assessment of the likelihood (qualitative probability) of such malevolent acts by adversaries;

- Evaluation of existing countermeasures; and

- Analysis of current risk and development of a prioritized plan for risk reduction.

Water Sector risk assessment tools enable drinking water and wastewater utilities to identify, inventory, and assess the criticality of utility-specific components in much greater detail. The attributes that contribute to a utility's security may include components central to its mission and function and of drinking water and wastewater utilities that span the physical plant, personnel, knowledge base, IT, and customers. Examples include intakes, collection systems, treatment plants, storage, chemicals, and distribution systems. Risk assessment tools developed for the Water Sector and supported by EPA funding or by others include:

- Risk Assessment Methodology for Water Utilities (RAM-W);

- Risk Assessment Methodology for small and medium utilities;

- Vulnerability Self-Assessment Tool (VSAT) for water, wastewater, and water/wastewater systems;

- Security and Emergency Management Systems;

- Security Vulnerability Self-Assessment Guide for small drinking water systems serving populations of 3,300 to 10,000;

- Security Vulnerability Self-Assessment Guide for very small drinking water systems serving populations of fewer than 3,300;

- Automated Security Survey and Evaluation Tool for small drinking water systems; and

- *Protecting Your Community's Assets: A Guide for Small Wastewater Systems.*

EPA has collaborated with Water Sector organizations to make these tools and associated training available to many utilities. Beyond the one-time requirements of the Bioterrorism Act, the Agency cannot require drinking water utilities serving fewer than 3,300 persons or any wastewater utility to conduct or submit vulnerability assessments. Along with its security partners, EPA encourages all utilities to conduct and revise risk assessments—especially as new and improved vulnerability, consequence, and threat information becomes available.

As of September 2006, EPA can verify that 100 percent of large (service populations greater than 100,000) and medium (service populations of 50,000 to 100,000) CWSs have conducted risk assessments and submitted ERPs. Ninety-eight percent of small CWSs (service populations of 3,301 to 49,999) have completed risk assessments, and 96 percent have created or updated ERPs. EPA continues to help smaller utilities develop risk assessments and ERPs through guidance and training.

2.1.6 Privacy of Data

The privacy of Water Sector data varies by database. Before 9/11, SDWIS and PCS were accessible online, and members of the public were encouraged to "surf your watershed" to obtain information from both databases. SDWIS information continues to be available to the general public, although access to the geographic coordinates of drinking water utilities is restricted. Identifying POTWs using the Integrated Compliance Information System database maintained by EPA's Office of Enforcement and Compliance Assurance is possible; however it is also possible to access latitude and longitude data for water systems that have chemicals on site through the Agency's Toxics Release Inventory database. Information from these databases and surveys also may be obtained through the Freedom of Information Act (FOIA). A benefit of FOIA is that its procedures allow information to be exempt from disclosure.

Water utilities expect that all data and information they provide voluntarily to the DHS or EPA will be protected from release by Protected Critical Infrastructure Information (PCII) classification or other appropriate classification procedures. The sector will work with the PCII Program to apply, to the extent possible, the provisions of the Critical Infrastructure Information (CII) Act of 2002 and to implement the final PCII rule, found at 6 Code of Federal Regulations (CFR) Part 29, to protect critical infrastructure information that is not customarily in the public domain and is voluntarily submitted to the DHS. EPA will not request or hold sensitive or critical information about Water Sector infrastructure beyond what it currently holds or collects unless and until it is able to protect this information from release. The Agency will use such information only for national CIP purposes. The Water Sector will also work with State, local, and tribal authorities to ensure that information provided to them is appropriately protected from release and used only for infrastructure protection. Until certification that the DHS information contained in the NADB will be shared only with those who "need to know," and that the information is protected from FOIA, EPA will not be able to provide additional information to the DHS for the NADB.

2.2 Verifying Infrastructure Information

Data verification is an ongoing process; much of the data collected by EPA that pertains to the Water Sector is subject to verification and validation protocols. EPA's databases and surveys have well-established quality control and verification procedures for data collection and data entry, including data screening, double-key entry, and logic checks. EPA conducts routine audits of State data at least once every four years using a formal audit process and data verification teams.

Upon receipt of a required Bioterrorism Act vulnerability (risk) assessment from a CWS, EPA's designated official reviewed the assessment to ensure the criteria defined in the Bioterrorism Act were included, and that the utility made a reasonable effort to develop a comprehensive assessment. If the submittal was incomplete, EPA contacted the individual(s) listed on the submittal package for clarification or additional information. Community drinking water systems subject to requirements of the Act were required to conduct a risk assessment only once. The Bioterrorism Act does not address updating assessments for these community systems, does not require smaller drinking water or any wastewater systems to conduct assessments, and does not require systems that have performed risk assessments to take actions based on the results.

When data verification processes are deemed inadequate, whether for the NADB or other CIP purposes, EPA will work with security expert groups, such as the WSCC and Water Sector associations, to identify and implement appropriate processes, including processes to verify security-related data. Data verification will often require involvement with an individual asset owner/operator. The sector will work to develop protocols to ensure that all data used for CIP are verified, fill a clearly identified void, meet mutually agreed-upon accuracy and completeness thresholds, and are essential to Water Sector infrastructure protection. In times of emergency or crisis, trusted communication channels between asset owner/operators and government and other security partners will ensure data quality.

2.3 Updating Infrastructure Information

By virtue of EPA's approach to meet its mission under the SDWA and CWA, two basic inventories for all Water Sector utilities, SDWIS and PCS, are updated routinely; other databases are updated at least every four years. EPA will work with its sector security partners to support regular updating of key Water Sector asset and infrastructure data, avoid duplication, reduce the burden of reporting by using advanced data collection technologies, and obtain regular updates on key infrastructure data that are not otherwise updated or reported. When deemed necessary for the security of the homeland and critical infrastructure, and while recognizing resource and time constraints, EPA will work with the sector to ensure more frequent updates of data or data elements. EPA currently is working with the DHS to determine how and how often Water Sector data will be updated for the NADB. A CIPAC Joint Working Group composed of representatives from the WSCC and GCC will be involved in development of these data criteria and will, as appropriate, provide input into the RAMCAP process.

3. Assess Risks

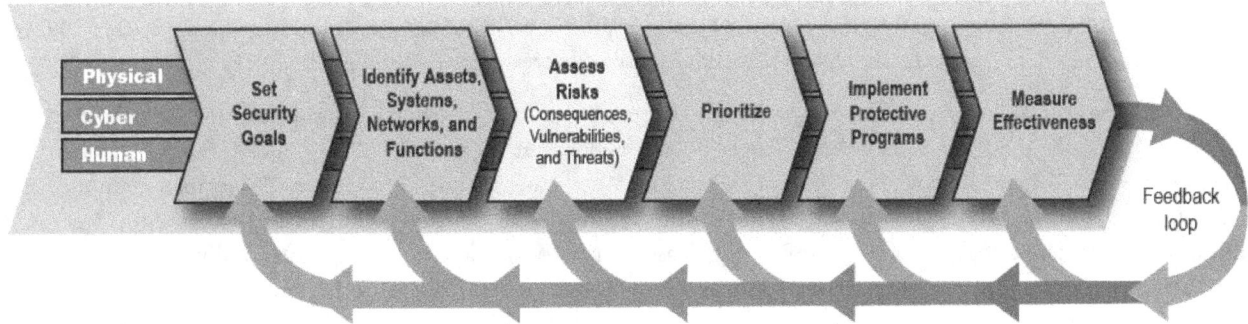

Continuous improvement to enhance protection of CI/KR

This section addresses the Water Sector's approach for assessing risk as defined in the NIPP. Risk is a measure of potential harm that encompasses threat, vulnerability, and consequence. An asset's risk is a function of its vulnerability to a disruption or attack, the likelihood of a disruption or attack (often referred to as the threat to the asset or the asset's attractiveness), and the likely consequences of a disruption or successful attack. This section also provides information on assessment methods that are unique to the sector, the process of evaluating the compatibility of existing methodologies with the RAMCAP criteria, implementation of risk assessments by the Water Sector, the roles of the partners in conducting risk assessments, and limitations on providing information to the DHS about the outcome of assessments. Important to note is that "vulnerability assessment" is the accepted terminology in the Water Sector due to the language of the Bioterrorism Act. The term is equivalent to the DHS's "risk assessment," since the methodologies developed for the Water Sector considered all the components of risk: consequence, threat, and vulnerability.

HSPD-7 requires the DHS to develop a program to identify, prioritize, and coordinate the protection of critical infrastructure in order to prevent, detect, respond to, and recover from the effects of deliberate acts against drinking water and wastewater assets. EPA, coordinating with its sector security partners, has developed a comprehensive program that includes a suite of risk assessment tools, training, research initiatives, outreach materials, and technical and financial assistance to help Water Sector assets identify and better protect their key components. This program's all-hazards approach includes protecting assets from natural disasters as well as terrorist or other intentional attacks. The initiatives and actions described in this section directly support all sector goals, especially Goal 2: Recognize and Reduce Risk in the Water Sector.

3.1 Use of Risk Assessment in Sector

The SDWA and CWA set a historical framework for protection of drinking water and wastewater assets. A well-established system, coordinated among EPA, State primacy agencies, and utilities, is in place to protect the public and environment from exposure to various types of contaminants that can adversely affect public health and the environment. This framework employs a multiple-barrier approach that involves source water protection, treatment, redundancy, monitoring, certified operators, and public notification. As part of this framework, many Water Sector assets developed ERPs to deal with intentional acts as well as natural disasters.

In response to the terrorist attacks of September 11, 2001, Congress passed the Bioterrorism Act. The law amended the SDWA to provide a more specific focus on protection of drinking water assets from terrorism and other malevolent acts. It required CWSs serving more than 3,300 persons to conduct vulnerability assessments and develop ERPs based on the findings. The CWs subject to the Bioterrorism Act serve more than 91 percent of the U.S. population that receives its potable water from publicly or privately owned water utilities. As of September 2006, EPA can verify that all the drinking water utilities serving populations greater than 50,000 have completed their risk assessments and ERPs. Ninety-eight percent of utilities serving 3,301 to 49,999 persons have completed risk assessments, and 96 percent of these have created or updated ERPs.

To assist with these assessments, several years ago EPA and its security partners provided probable baseline threat information for drinking water and wastewater utilities. The DHS, in collaboration with the CIA, FBI, and EPA, recently created a Joint Strategic Sector Threat Assessment for Drinking Water and Wastewater Utilities. More detailed information on the baseline threat information and Strategic Sector Threat Assessment is provided in the "Assessing Threat" section of this section. Furthermore, the Water Sector developed a number of risk assessment tools to assist drinking water and wastewater utilities become better prepared to prevent, detect, respond to, and recover from terrorist attacks, other intentional acts, natural disasters, and other hazards. Because of the diversity of assets in the Water Sector (e.g., size, treatment complexity, disinfection practices), a multitude of risk assessment methodologies were created and are used. These tools address the full range of utility components, including the physical plant (physical), employees (human), IT (cyber), communications, and customers. These tools were developed for drinking water and wastewater utilities of all sizes; the elements of the risk assessments are outlined in the box below.

Elements of Water Sector Vulnerability (Risk) Assessments

These elements of a Water Sector vulnerability (risk) assessment are conceptual; they are not intended to serve as a detailed methodology.

• Characterization of the asset, including its mission and objectives;

• Identification and prioritization of adverse consequences to avoid;

• Determination of critical components that might be subject to malevolent acts that could result in undesired consequences;

• Assessment of the likelihood (qualitative probability) of such malevolent acts by adversaries;

• Evaluation of existing countermeasures; and

• Analysis of current risk and development of a prioritized plan for risk reduction.

An evaluation of these vulnerability assessments will be initiated in the RAMCAP process to assess their compatibility with the DHS's criteria for risk assessments and to take into consideration the DHS's common definitions and analysis of these basic risk factors:

- **Consequence (C) Analysis**, which is the estimate of the potential public health and economic impacts that a successful attack could cause;

- **Vulnerability (V) Assessment**, which identifies weaknesses in an asset design, implementation, or operation that can be exploited by an adversary; and

- **Threat (T) Analysis**, which estimates the likelihood that a particular target, or type of target, will be selected for attack, and is based on intent and capability of an adversary.

When these three factors are combined, they form the risk associated with an asset. The result is a comprehensive, systematic, and defensible assessment of an asset that drives integrated risk reduction activities. Risk assessments do more than address terrorist threats; by using the all-hazards approach, they allow for a more complete suite of integrated risk-reduction activities.

Figure 3-1: Calculating Risk

$$\text{Risk (R)} = f\{\text{Consequence (C)} \times \text{Threat (T)} \times \text{Vulnerability(V)}\}$$

To facilitate drinking water risk assessments, EPA made grant funds available to the Nation's largest drinking water utilities, those with service populations greater than 100,000. EPA also continues to provide funding to State primacy agencies to assist small and medium systems, and it has helped fund and develop a variety of Web casts and security trainings.

Although drinking water systems serving 3,300 or fewer persons and all wastewater systems were not required to conduct risk assessments, EPA, in collaboration with its Water Sector security partners, continues to encourage and support the conduct and revision of these assessments and ERPs by drinking water and wastewater utilities of all sizes. This support is provided through development of risk assessment tools, training, and assistance.

In addition, EPA and many of its sector security partners have provided many security-related training workshops on such topics as risk assessment methodologies, ERPs, and tabletop exercises. These training sessions have been well attended by utilities of all sizes.

While EPA and its security partners developed various risk assessment tools at the national level, Water Sector owner/operators are responsible for conducting the analyses. Each assessment was conducted at the asset-level with vulnerability, consequence, and threat analyses associated with the various components of each asset. Because each assessment is based on local conditions, threats, and factors such as asset complexity and number of persons served, the approach and results of an assessment vary for each asset.

As noted previously, the results of the vulnerability assessments mandated by the Bioterrorism Act are protected, and access is limited to individuals designated by the EPA Administrator. Specifically, the Bioterrorism Act states:

- Each copy of such assessment, and all information contained in or derived from the assessment, is kept in a secure location;

- Only individuals designated by the Administrator may have access to the copies of the assessments; and

- No copy of an assessment or part of an assessment, or information contained in or derived from an assessment shall be available to anyone other than an individual designated by the Administrator.

Currently EPA is not able to protect sensitive data with the exception of the authorities under the Bioterrorism Act; while EPA can work with the Water Sector and encourage data submittal; it does not have the authority to require risk assessments. The DHS has in place the PCII Program and final rule, which have been designed to enable it to protect sensitive information that is voluntarily submitted from private sector entities. Federal agencies need to work together to examine the applicability of the PCII rule in the Water Sector to ensure that sensitive information submitted to the DHS through the PCII Program is properly protected.

A set of baseline criteria for the methodologies used to support all levels of comparative risk analyses is defined in appendix 3A of the NIPP Base Plan. The Water Sector will consider such criteria as it evaluates how best to move forward in terms of risk assessments that will support the DHS's national comparative risk analysis goals. The sector concurs with the DHS's stated objective of using previous assessments whenever possible to support such analyses.

3.2 Assessing Consequences

The potential consequences of any incident, including a terrorist attack and natural or manmade disaster, are the first factor to be considered in risk assessment. In the context of the NIPP, consequence is measured as the range of loss or damage that can be expected.

The consequences considered for the national comparative risk assessment are based on the criteria set forth in HSPD-7. These criteria can be divided into four main categories:

- **Health impact:** Effect on human life and physical well-being;

- **Economic impact:** Effect on the local, State, territorial, tribal, regional, or national economy;

- **Psychological impact:** Effect on the public's morale and confidence in national economic and political institutions; and

- **Governance impact:** Effect on the national government's ability to maintain order, deliver minimum essential public services, ensure public heath and safety, and carry out national security missions.

Consequences can be measured either quantitatively or qualitatively. Health and economic impacts generally lend themselves to quantitative measurement (e.g., number of lives lost; cost in dollars of rebuilding an asset), whereas psychological and governance impacts are more often measured qualitatively. Factors to consider in assessing the consequences of any disruption of a Water Sector asset include the:

- Magnitude of service disruption;

- Number of illnesses or deaths resulting from an event;

- Impact on public confidence;

- Chronic problems arising from specific events;

- Economic impacts; and

- Other indicators of the impact of each event, as determined by the utility.

Understanding the potential impacts and magnitude of disruption if a Water Sector asset is lost or compromised is vital. While a drinking water utility may be able to recover relatively quickly if one of its non-critical components is rendered inoperable, the loss of a critical component or the entire asset may result in significant consequences that cover all four categories of concern: health, economic, psychological, and governance. Denial of drinking water service means that people cannot cook, bathe, or flush toilets; fires cannot be fought; hospitals and other medical services will not be able to operate fully; and industries that depend on water will be shut down.

Consequences of concern can also include the public health and economic impacts resulting from loss of a wastewater asset's services. Not only can release of untreated sewage into rivers, lakes, and reservoirs cause environmental damage, it can also affect drinking water treatment plants downstream that draw their raw water from these sources.

The magnitude of the ultimate impacts will depend on how long service is lost (i.e., 1 hour, 3 days, or 3 weeks). Recent incidents such as the 2003 Northeast blackout and Hurricane Katrina provide a telling picture of the impacts and devastation that can result when a water utility is compromised and water taken for granted is no longer available. These dependencies and interdependencies are critical and must be understood and addressed by the Water Sector, DHS, and those services and other critical infrastructures that depend on a constant supply of safe drinking water and uninterrupted provision of wastewater treatment.

The consequences of significant concern for a drinking water utility depend on its design and could include:

- **Loss of supply for fire suppression or potable water for a significant part of the utility** (i.e., tap water will not be available for drinking, cooking, bathing, flushing toilets, or fighting fires);

- **Long-term loss of supply, treatment, or distribution** (i.e., residential customers who may be out of water for days, weeks, or months will have to find or be provided alternative sources of water for drinking, cooking, bathing, and flushing toilets; businesses may not have access to the water they need to operate);

- **Catastrophic release of on-site hazardous chemicals that affects public health** (i.e., significant loss of life in the immediate area of the release and evacuation of large numbers of persons from the surrounding areas);

- **Adverse impacts to public health or confidence from actual or threatened intentional contamination of water with biological, chemical, or radiological materials** (i.e., the public will fear using its water because of concerns it might not be safe, thus necessitating alternative sources of water for an unspecified period of time; questions about the safety of the distribution system after decontamination may also be raised); and

- **Adverse economic and environmental impacts** (i.e., industries that use water may be shut down; utilities or local governments may have to provide alternative sources of water for drinking, cooking, and bathing; loss of water for irrigation could affect the food supply and production of staples).

The consequences of significant concern for a wastewater utility depend on its design and could include:

- **Collateral damage to buildings, institutions, and icons that could result in loss of life by using the sanitary or storm water collection systems to gain access to these facilities** (i.e., collection systems can serve as conduits to other critical infrastructure);

- **Long-term loss of collection or treatment and resulting impacts to drinking water sources** (i.e., untreated sewage released to receiving waters can create public health and treatment issues for downstream drinking water systems);

- **Catastrophic release of stored hazardous chemicals, affecting public health** (i.e., significant loss of life in the immediate area of the release and evacuation of large numbers of persons from the surrounding areas);

- **Decontamination of wastewater and subsequent residual disposal** (i.e., contaminated wastewater may have to be pretreated before it can go through a wastewater treatment plant, particularly one with biological treatment; the potential hazardous residual remaining after treatment must be disposed of safely); and

- **Adverse economic and environmental impacts** (i.e., release of untreated sewage could cause loss or destruction of plants, animals, and aquatic life; without basic sanitation capabilities, services such as hospitals and some industries may not be able to function).

EPA has moved toward identifying the consequences of an attack by applying the CARVER + Shock methodology to learn the public health and economic impacts; however, this analysis is limited to the potential impacts of contamination on a drinking water distribution system and does not consider the compounding or independent impacts of a physical or cyber attack.

Therefore, in collaboration with its Water Sector security partners, EPA will next analyze the human health and economic consequences of potential scenarios at drinking water and wastewater utilities. This effort will help to provide utilities with better consequence analysis information so they can conduct more informed risk assessments. It also will help raise the awareness of others (e.g., Federal, State, and local governments and the intelligence community) about risks in the Water Sector. This project will meet one of EPA's Implementation Actions identified in appendix 2B of the NIPP. Five major steps will be taken: (1) define threat/vulnerability scenarios; (2) define probable responses; (3) assess human health consequences; (4) assess economic consequences; and (5) implement a pilot project to verify results of analysis.

Reliance on another asset or sector for the functioning of certain assets is called a dependency; if two assets depend on one another, they are called interdependent. EPA has undertaken numerous analyses to better understand and evaluate the dependencies and interdependencies between the Water Sector and other infrastructure sectors. Interdependencies within the Water Sector and among the other CI/KR sectors must be considered when discussing consequences. These interdependencies may have local, regional, or national implications. They are considered to be essential elements of a comprehensive examination of physical and cyber vulnerabilities. In addition, the Water Sector's increasing reliance on cyber systems (e.g., process control systems), coupled with the downsizing of the sector workforce, has resulted in critical dependency on certain highly skilled human resources.

Recent events including hurricanes and blackouts have provided numerous lessons and real-life examples of interdependencies. By definition, infrastructure interdependencies transcend individual sectors and may transcend individual companies. Further, they vary in scale and complexity, ranging from local linkages (e.g., municipal water supply systems and local emergency services) to regional linkages (e.g., electric power coordinating councils), national linkages (e.g., interstate natural gas and transportation systems), and international linkages (e.g., communications, banking, and financial systems). The scale and complexity differences create spatial, temporal, and system representation complexities. Each link in the water/wastewater infrastructure has important, and potentially different, spatial, temporal, and utility characteristics. These dependencies and interdependencies are taken into consideration when utilities conduct their consequence analyses as part of the risk assessment process.

Interdependencies historically have been considered to be either physical or geographic. For example, the water and power sectors are integrally and often physically linked: the Water Sector needs power to operate its pumps and treatment operations, while the power sector often depends on the Water Sector for cooling water. Geographic interdependencies arise when infrastructure components (e.g., water pipelines, conveyance lines, gas pipelines, and telecommunications cables) share common corridors, thus increasing the vulnerabilities to and consequences of all hazards.

The increased use of automated monitoring and control systems and SCADA systems has increased the interdependencies among infrastructures. Furthermore, greater use of the open market for buying and selling some infrastructure commodities and services has also increased the interdependencies. Preparing for and responding to incidents involving critical infrastructures requires that interdependent events and impacts be properly identified and assessed.

Figure 3-2 illustrates some of the interdependencies of the drinking water infrastructure with the transportation, health care, natural gas, petroleum liquids, communications, emergency management services (EMS), and electric power infrastructures. Similar comparisons could be made illustrating the dependence of wastewater systems on other infrastructures, and the dependency of other infrastructures on critical Water Sector infrastructure.

Figure 3-2: Interdependencies With the Water Sector

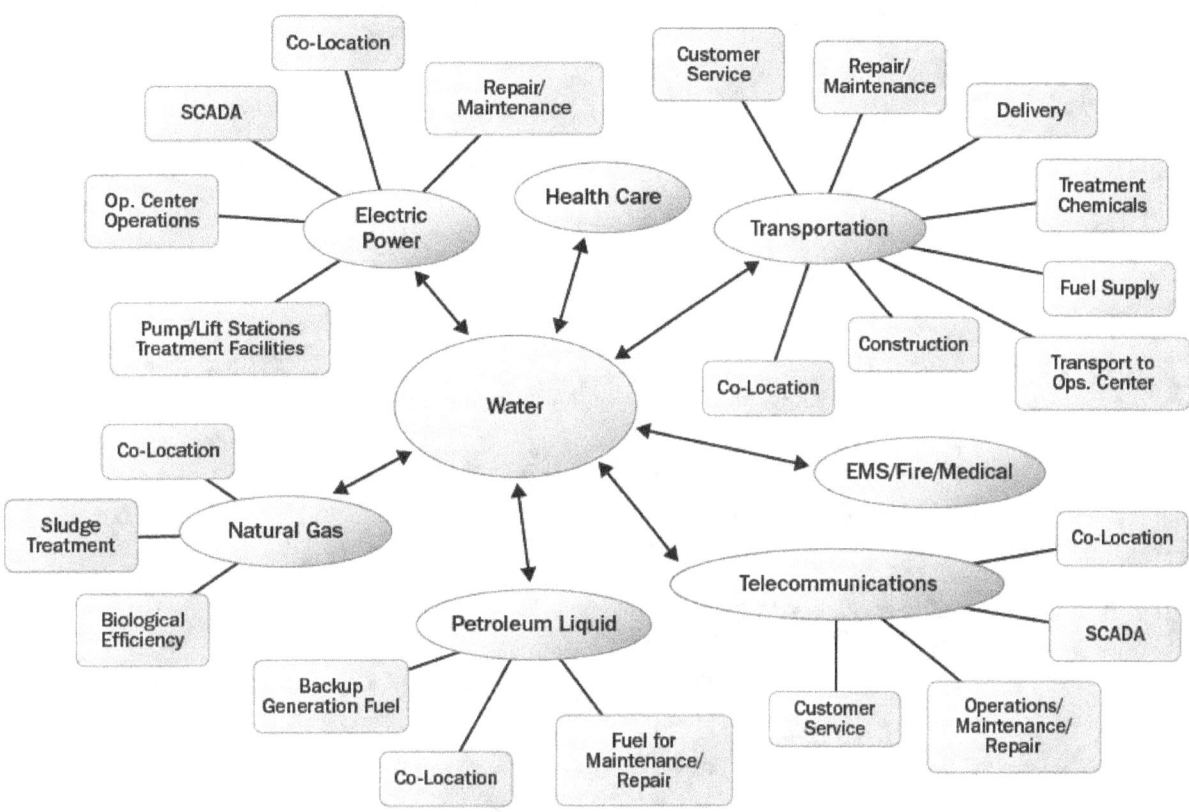

Interdependencies between drinking water utilities and other critical infrastructures are shown in table 3-1. The preliminary data gathered for this exhibit are not meant to illustrate an exhaustive list of interdependencies; rather, they capture some of the broader concerns.

Table 3-1: Interdependencies Between Sectors and Water Supply

Infrastructure	Infrastructure Dependency on Drinking Water	Drinking Water Dependency on Infrastructure
Agriculture	• Irrigation* • Animal drinking • Facility cleaning	
Food	• Food processing • Restaurant operation	

Infrastructure	Infrastructure Dependency on Drinking Water	Drinking Water Dependency on Infrastructure
Public Health and Health Care	• Hospital/clinic operations • Nursing home operations • Pharmaceutical, device, and supply manufacturing • Laboratory services • Transportation of equipment and supplies	
Emergency Services	• Firefighting • Emergency water supplies • Equipment maintenance	• Coordination with emergency responders
Government	• Office operations	• Water rates and spending authority • Research
Defense Industrial Base	• Office operations • Equipment cooling	• Production of parts
Communications	• Equipment cooling • Common rights-of-way	• General operations • SCADA • Remote monitoring • Communication with emergency responders • Common rights-of-way
Energy	• Steam generation • Mining operations • Ore processing • Refining • Pollution control • Raw material (e.g., hydrogen production) • Waste management • Common rights-of-way • Office operations	• Pumps, wells, treatment, etc. operations and repair • Office operations • Common rights-of-way • Repair/recovery operations • Delivery of components, materials • Backup power requirements

Infrastructure	Infrastructure Dependency on Drinking Water	Drinking Water Dependency on Infrastructure
Transportation	• Office operations • Equipment maintenance • Common rights-of-way	• Delivery of treatment chemicals • Operations, maintenance, repair • Delivery of components, materials • Company operations • Transport of emergency responders and equipment • Common rights-of-way
Banking and Finance	• Office operations • Equipment cooling	• Company operations
Chemical Industry and Hazardous Materials	• Manufacturing operations • Office operations	• Chlorine and other treatment chemicals
Postal and Shipping	• Office operations	• Company operations
National Monuments and Icons	• Office operations • Provision of public facilities	

*The most common sources of water for irrigation include rivers, reservoirs and lakes, and groundwater.

Table 3-1 shows that most of the interdependencies other infrastructures have with water are physical in nature. That is, these infrastructures require water to provide products or services. Geographic interdependencies seen between water infrastructure and other infrastructures are due to the practice of placing water pipelines, electricity lines, telecommunication lines, etc. in common corridors.

Water is an unusual commodity in that it is continually used and reused. The water taken in by a supplier may have been treated and discharged by a user upstream. This situation creates a unique intradependency among individual water or wastewater utilities. As previously noted, if the upstream dischargers are not sufficiently prepared for emergencies, they might release untreated or insufficiently treated water into a river that is the raw water source for a downstream water supplier. Because the design and operation of the downstream drinking water treatment facility is predicated on the raw water being of a certain quality, the facility conceivably cannot adequately treat the water under these conditions. In such cases, the treated water might not meet health standards.

Table 3-2 shows the interdependencies between wastewater infrastructure and other critical infrastructures. As is the case with drinking water interdependencies, most of the wastewater interdependencies are physical. One of the growing uses of treated wastewater is to cool electric power-generating stations. To compensate for limited water resources, facility designers are looking to alternative water sources. The preliminary data gathered for this exhibit are not meant to illustrate an exhaustive list of interdependencies; rather, they capture some of the broader concerns.

Table 3-2: Interdependencies Between Sectors and Wastewater Infrastructure

Infrastructure	Infrastructure Dependency on Drinking Water	Drinking Water Dependency on Infrastructure
Agriculture	• Biosolids (soil amendment/fertilizer)	• Biosolids disposal
Food	• Restaurant operation • Processing plants	
Public Health and Health Care	• Hospital/clinic operations • Nursing home operations • Pharmaceutical, device, and supply manufacturing • Laboratory services • Transportation of equipment and supplies	
Emergency Services	• Decontamination services	• Coordination with emergency responders
Government	• Office operations	• Water rates and spending authority • Research
Defense Industrial Base	• Office operations	• Production of parts
Communications	• Common rights-of-way	• General operations • SCADA • Remote monitoring • Communication with emergency responders • Common rights-of-way

Infrastructure	Infrastructure Dependency on Drinking Water	Drinking Water Dependency on Infrastructure
Energy	• Waste management • Common rights-of-way • Methane generation • Cooling water	• Pumps, treatment, etc. operations and repair • Office operations • Common rights-of-way • Repair/recovery operations • Delivery of components, materials • Backup power requirements
Transportation	• Office operations • Common rights-of-way	• Delivery of treatment chemicals • Operations, maintenance, repair • Delivery of components, materials • Company operations • Transport of emergency responders and equipment • Common rights-of-way
Banking and Finance	• Office operations	• Company operations
Chemical Industry and Hazardous Materials	• Manufacturing operations • Office operations	• Chlorine and other treatment chemicals
Postal and Shipping	• Office operations	• Company operations
National Monuments and Icons	• Office operations • Provision of public facilities	

EPA plans to continue working with the Water Sector to evaluate models and computer simulations that may provide more information about interdependencies, and to promote rapid response, repair, and recovery from attacks. When work is completed, information regarding the sector's interdependency concerns will be shared with other affected SSAs so that appropriate planning can occur.

3.3 Assessing Vulnerabilities

Vulnerabilities are the characteristics of an asset's design, location, security posture, process, and operation that make it susceptible to destruction, incapacitation, or exploitation by mechanical failures, natural hazards, terrorist attacks, or other malicious acts. They identify weaknesses that could result in consequences of concern, taking into account intrinsic structural weaknesses, protective measures, resiliency, and redundancies. As noted earlier, all risk assessment methodologies developed for the Water Sector will be evaluated to determine their compatibility with the RAMCAP criteria and therefore with the DHS's national risk management framework.

EPA and its Water Sector security partners have developed risk assessment tools for drinking water and wastewater utilities of different sizes. Below are descriptions of the tools developed for the water sector.

Risk Assessment Methodology for Water Utilities (RAM-W). This comprehensive security risk assessment methodology was designed for large drinking water utilities. It covers all aspects of water utility operations. Extensive fault trees throughout the analysis help the utility systematically assess its vulnerabilities to attack. The results provide a prioritized list of relative risks to be considered for system or security upgrades.

Risk Assessment Methodology for Small and Medium Drinking Water Utilities. This streamlined version of RAM-W provides step-by-step instructions for assessing risk:

1. Determining the important utility components to protect;

2. Determining the consequences of losing key components;

3. Defining the types of threats and likelihood of their occurrence;

4. Defining safeguards to protect the utility from sabotage;

5. Analyzing the utility to determine constraints; and

6. Developing an ERP to counter or minimize risks.

Interdependencies with other sectors, employee screening, security policies, and contingency plans are also addressed.

VSAT: Water, Water/Wastewater, and Wastewater. This software tool for drinking water, combined drinking water and wastewater, and wastewater utilities of all sizes includes a comprehensive CD-ROM package that enables utilities to:

- Assess their vulnerability;

- Determine potential solutions for the prioritized vulnerabilities;

- Develop priorities for security improvements; and

- Plan for emergency responses.

The tool covers the full range of utility components, including physical plant, employees, IT, communications, and customers. Its threat library contains information on manmade disruptions and natural disasters that utilities can apply to determine their potential consequences to each system component. Upon completion of the assessment, the software provides the user with a vulnerability assessment report and updated ERP.

Self-Assessment Guide for Small Drinking Water Systems Serving Populations Between 3,300 and 10,000. This vulnerability assessment guide provides a streamlined tool for small drinking water utilities as they inventory their critical components, conduct self-assessments, and prioritize needed actions.

Security and Emergency Management System. This software tool for drinking water utilities serving between 3,300 and 10,000 persons is based on the Self-Assessment Guide for Small Drinking Water Systems Serving Populations Between 3,300 and 10,000. The CD-ROM provides a step-by-step process for evaluating a water utility and developing a vulnerability assessment. Upon completion of the assessment, the software provides the user with a vulnerability assessment report and updated ERP.

Self-Assessment Guide for Very Small (< 3,300) Systems. This guide performs the same function as the preceding tool, but is tailored for utilities serving fewer than 3,300 persons.

Automated Security Survey and Evaluation Tool. This self-guided software program is designed to assist small and medium drinking water utilities complete vulnerability assessments and improve their security and preparedness for dealing with a range of threats.

Protecting Your Community's Assets: A Guide for Small Wastewater Systems. This guide for wastewater utilities that serve populations of less than 10,000 takes utility managers, operators, and local officials through a vulnerability assessment to improve security and plan for emergencies affecting wastewater treatment utilities.

More information about these risk assessment tools can be found at EPA's Security Web site (http://cfpub.epa/safewater/water-security/home.cfm?program_id=11).

3.4 Assessing Threats

The Water Sector views threat analysis broadly, encompassing natural events, criminal acts, insider threats, and foreign and domestic terrorism. Natural events are typically addressed as part of emergency response and business continuity planning. In order to conduct a meaningful risk assessment, the threat component of risk analysis is calculated based on the likelihood that an asset will be disrupted or attacked. Therefore, the Water Sector strongly believes that relevant and timely threat information must be disseminated whenever possible prior to conducting (and to inform) risk assessments. A number of sector representatives, including most members of the WSCC and GCC, hold national security clearances that facilitate sharing of such classified threat information. In addition, the WaterISAC and WaterSC facilitate communications among sector owner/operators, security stakeholders, the Federal Government, and other critical infrastructures. The WaterISAC serves as a conduit for disseminating sensitive risk and incident information.

In 2006, the DHS started a national initiative, the Strategic Homeland Infrastructure Risk Assessment, to help all 17 CI/KR SSAs assess risk. This assessment is conducted in part with the SSA; the SSA determines vulnerabilities and consequences, and the DHS determines threat. The DHS has identified 15 different threat themes that have implications for the Nation's critical infrastructure sectors. Several themes directly apply to the Water Sector:

- Chemical, biological, or radiological (CBR) contamination attacks on drinking water assets, especially distribution systems;

- Vehicle-borne improvised explosive devices and improvised explosive device attacks on infrastructure, especially single points of failure and chemical storage sites;

- Cyber attacks on industrial control systems; and

- Chemical attacks, which may include introduction of a combustible contaminant into a wastewater collection system, affecting infrastructure or the treatment process.

This assessment also examines protective actions and, to a lesser extent, needs in relationship to these threat themes.

To assist Water Sector utilities conduct risk assessments, EPA has developed the Drinking Water and Wastewater Baseline Threat Documents. The Bioterrorism Act required EPA to develop and provide baseline threat information to CWSs by August 1, 2002, to aid them in performing vulnerability assessments. The Agency developed the Baseline Threat Information for Vulnerability Assessments of Community Water Systems (baseline threat document) in consultation with many stakeholders. The document gives utilities information to: (1) undertake risk-based vulnerability assessments of their asset components; (2) analyze potential threats; and (3) consider potential modes of attack. The document lists vulnerability assessment tools and other information resources to help water utilities learn more about threats in their areas. To control the circulation of the baseline threat document, EPA established a protocol for water utilities to follow in order to obtain a copy.

Wastewater utilities are reassessing their ability to provide secure and reliable service to customers and communities. While there are no requirements for wastewater systems to conduct risk assessments, some have already done so. They undertook the risk assessments to assure their governing boards, customers, and community that they:

• Thoroughly understand their vulnerabilities and the risks associated with them;

• Have addressed these vulnerabilities in their ERPs, which are in place and regularly tested; and

• Have plans and programs to guide their recovery from a crisis, thereby minimizing impacts on their customers and community.

To assist wastewater utilities, WEF, with support from EPA and many Water Sector security partners, created in June 2005 the Wastewater Baseline Threat Document. The document provides guidance to wastewater utilities on:

• Understanding their systems' vulnerabilities and related threats;

• Identifying approaches for risk-based assessments of their assets; and

• Understanding the planning steps to perform an assessment.

It also gives wastewater utilities information to:

• Undertake risk-based vulnerability assessments of their asset's components;

• Analyze potential threats; and

• Consider potential modes of attack.

The document also lists vulnerability assessment tools and other information resources to help wastewater systems learn more about threats in their areas.

Determining the magnitude of all possible terrorist threats is beyond the scope of most non-Federal (and many Federal) entities. Consequently, most asset owner/operators must rely on threat information from the DHS and Federal and local law enforcement to accurately calculate the relative risk associated with a given asset. The DHS's Homeland Infrastructure Threat and Risk Analysis Center (HITRAC), which conducts integrated threat analyses for all CI/KR sectors, must work in partnership with owner/operators to ensure that suitable threat information is made available. The same genuine partnership must also exist at all levels of local, State, and Federal law enforcement.

Under the NIPP, HITRAC is responsible for producing assessments that support strategic planning by the owner/operators of critical infrastructure to enhance the protection and preparedness of all national CI/KR. HITRAC analyzes information about terrorist objectives and attack capabilities, and compares these analyses against vulnerability and consequence assessments to assess potential terrorist attack profiles that may be used against each CI/KR sector. This process yields a well-informed estimate of a threat that supplements specific intelligence and warnings regarding particular targets, attack vectors, or timing.

To provide the Water Sector with the most up-to-date threat-related data, HITRAC, in collaboration with EPA, CIA and FBI, has prepared, and the DHS has recently released, a Joint Strategic Sector Threat Assessment for Drinking Water and Wastewater Utilities. The document assesses the potential terrorist threats against the Nation's critical Water Sector infrastructure. The information is based on current threat information in the sector and builds on the Agency's baseline threat documents.

In addition to the Strategic Sector Threat Assessment, the Water Sector requests that, when applicable, HITRAC provide specific threat information based on real-time intelligence streams, which will help drive short-term protective measures to mitigate risk. The Water Sector would also benefit from:

- Periodic conference calls with asset owner/operators to relay recently reported suspicious activities near Water Sector facilities and other pertinent, unclassified, threat-related information;

- Analyses of suspicious activities reported near Water Sector facilities;

- Classified threat briefings for representatives of the sector; various Federal agencies would use these data to inform representatives about general and specific threats associated with the sector, as well as the overall threat of terrorism to the Nation; and

- Improved communications and increased participation with local and regional joint terrorism task forces.

While these forums and materials do not directly feed development of risk scores for Water Sector assets, they do provide valuable insight to security partners regarding the overall threat to the sector. More specifically, they help utilities, local law enforcement, and others to be more aware of potential indicators of terrorist or criminal activity.

3.5 Screening Infrastructure

As noted previously, the Water Sector is diverse and contains more than 53,000 CWSs and more than 16,000 wastewater utilities. The Bioterrorism Act explicitly required all drinking water systems serving more than 3,300 persons to conduct vulnerability (risk) assessments. These assessments were to help drinking water utilities evaluate their susceptibility to threats and identify corrective actions that might reduce or mitigate the risk of serious consequences of adversarial actions.

The Water Sector does not use a formal screening process to identify which assets should or should not perform risk assessments. EPA, in collaboration with the sector, continues to encourage all utilities to take security concerns into consideration. The different risk assessment methodologies developed for use by utility owner/operators allow them to choose the methodology most applicable to their security requirements depending on utility size, treatment method, and population served.

Given the large number of Water Sector utilities throughout the Nation and the limited resources available to address their security, the objective of the RAMCAP process is to prioritize at the national level those sector assets that warrant more in-depth risk analyses. The entire sector, especially owner/operators, may benefit from coordination within the sector on development of a screening process to determine the need for detailed risk assessments. Risk assessments are iterative; therefore, exploring development of screening methodologies could help identify assets that are significant enough to require further assessment. Because not all utilities face the same level of risk, the sector may want to limit more detailed assessments to only those assets with the highest risk. Specifically, a screening process that may use a standard form containing a few simple questions could be developed in collaboration with Water Sector security partners, EPA, and DHS. The screening would enable owner/operators to quickly look at potential consequences associated with attacks on theirs asset and determine whether those consequences are significant enough to warrant additional assessments.

Some risk assessment methodologies employ simplified and inexpensive-to-use consequence screening, or "top-screen", to help owner/operators decide whether a full risk assessment is necessary. If this initial screening determines that an attack is unlikely to result in significant consequences, owner/operators might want to reconsider more detailed assessments.

The Water Sector, DHS, and EPA are discussing how to coordinate development of a top-screen for the Water Sector and how to examine existing risk assessment methodologies to ensure their compatibility with RAMCAP or other sector methodologies. The RAMCAP framework satisfies the NIPP baseline criteria for risk assessment and can be used for national cross-sector risk assessment. It enables owner/operators to calculate vulnerability to an attack and the potential consequences using a consistent system of measurements. RAMCAP also will provide the means to convert and compare the results of assessments performed with other suitable methodologies that are consistent with the NIPP baseline criteria. At this time, the Water Sector is only considering engaging in a process to reevaluate its existing risk assessment methodologies for compatibility with RAMCAP. Sector security partners are willing to examine existing risk assessment methodologies to assist the DHS in cross-sector CI/KR asset comparisons. The process for these activities will involve development of a RAMCAP work group composed of representatives from WSCC and GCC, in addition to subject matter experts.

The Water Sector may benefit from examining existing risk assessment tools and methodologies against the NIPP baseline criteria. Such a review might help to ensure that the tools provide results that are suitable for national risk analyses, which rely on assessments that are comparable within and across sectors. These tools would be used to identify which assets would warrant expenditure of additional resources to conduct comprehensive risk assessments. While using screening tools as a precursor to in-depth risk assessments is an important step forward, the sector will engage with DHS to begin to develop a process that will define high-consequence assets in the sector; this process is described in more detail in section 4.

4. Prioritize Infrastructure

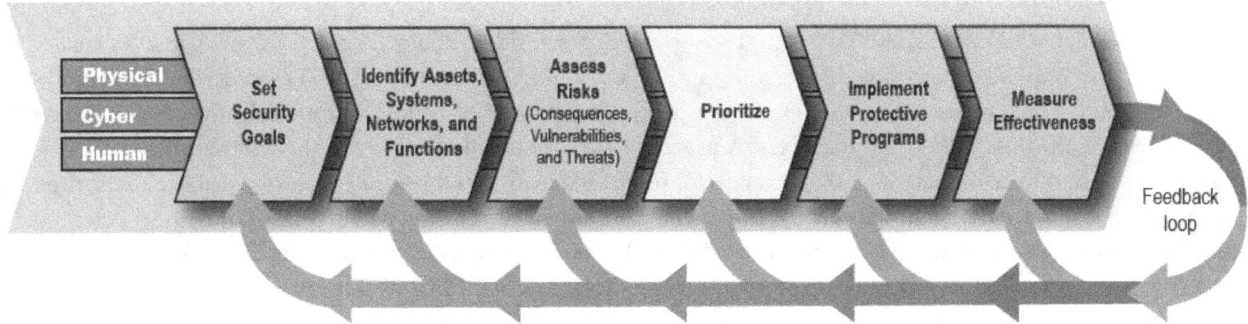

Continuous improvement to enhance protection of CI/KR

This section provides information on how Water Sector security partners plan to address the development process for risk-based prioritization of assets. As part of the national comparative risk assessment described in section 3.4 of the NIPP, prioritization across sectors (in support of national protective efforts) is performed by the DHS. Sectors are being asked to provide risk assessment information in a manner that is comparable with DHS risk management efforts in order to support the national comparative risk assessment. Section 3 of the SSP describes the process and the Water Sector's limitations in supporting this alignment.

For purposes of this section of the SSP, EPA reiterates that drinking water and wastewater assets are defined as entire utilities for purposes of identification, prioritization, and coordination in the Water Sector. Individual owner/operators are responsible for conducting risk assessments to identify the components of their utilities (e.g., pumps, generators, and SCADA systems) that are of higher consequence and concern if affected by manmade or natural events.

4.1 Asset Level Prioritization

Owner/operators of Water Sector assets have implicit screening processes to identify internal priorities related to business conditions, treatment, drinking water distribution, and reliability of wastewater collection to help them ensure continuity of operations. The importance of many components in a utility is highly variable and may depend on many considerations, including location and redundancy. Identification of a critical component of an asset is characterized by highly variable threats, consequences, and vulnerabilities. Many of the Nation's Water Sector assets are built with redundancy; the degree of redundancy varies from utility to utility across the country. The sector has well-developed protocols, organizations, and communication systems to help ensure the reliability of treatment, drinking water supply, and wastewater collection. EPA, the DHS, and Water Sector owners/operators and security partners will continue to work together to develop better threat, vulnerability, and consequence information to help utilities identify the most critical components of their systems.

4.2 Strategic Considerations

The Water Sector's approach to prioritizing protection efforts—so that resources are applied where they offer the most benefit, reducing risk by deterring threats and minimizing consequences of attacks—is consistent with the goals of the DHS national CIP program. A systematic and consistent way of prioritizing assets also offers transparency and increases the defensibility of the decisions made about resource allocation. To allocate resources in a manner that most cost-effectively reduces risk; protective efforts (e.g., activities, measures, programs) must be assessed and prioritized. This process gives decision makers information they can use to make policy, funding, and other decisions about CI/KR protection. The process used to prioritize protective programs, which is based on a combination of their risk reduction potential and cost effectiveness, is described in section 5.

The DHS is supporting development of RAMCAP, a risk assessment process that would allow the risk of an asset in a particular sector to be compared to the risk associated with other, similar assets from different sector(s). This process will use the widely accepted equation that determines risk by multiplying the likely consequences of a successful attack by the asset's vulnerability to attack, and by the likelihood of an attack on that particular asset. As noted elsewhere in this SSP, the DHS and EPA are discussing how to start to coordinate with the Water Sector on development of a screening process to determine the need for detailed risk assessments (top-screen) for Water Sector assets. They also are discussing how to examine existing sector risk assessment methodologies to ensure their compatibility with other methodologies so that the DHS can make cross-sector asset comparisons. WSCC and GCC have been presented with the RAMCAP concept, and a working group is being established by the DHS Risk Management Division under work that is being led by ASME (formerly known as the American Society of Mechanical Engineers).

To assist in this matter, EPA, in collaboration with its Water Sector security partners and the DHS, will begin to develop a process to define higher consequence assets in the sector. The security partners will work together to determine high-consequence asset elements. WSCC and GCC will help outline the process through which these elements will be identified. Several of the draft applicable elements for identifying higher consequence assets in the sector have been discussed, but they have not been fully vetted in the sector.

5. Implementing Protective Programs

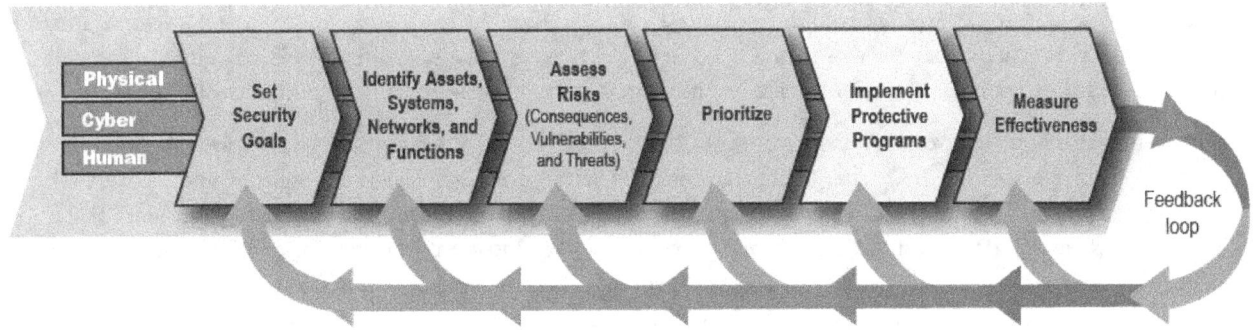

Continuous improvement to enhance protection of CI/KR

This section addresses how the Water Sector develops and implements protective programs that are used throughout the sector. A protective program is defined as a coordinated plan of action to prevent, deter, and mitigate terrorist attacks on critical assets, and respond to and recover from such attacks as quickly and effectively as possible. As stated in the NIPP, and as implemented by the Water Sector, protective programs also encompass an all-hazards approach that addresses not only a terrorist threat but natural disasters and other hazards. Protective programs guide infrastructure owner/operators on the most effective strategies for protecting their assets, including critical components, given the general classes of threats that are applicable to their system and their specific vulnerabilities. This section will focus on efforts to identify, assess, select, and implement protective programs and EPA's role in facilitating implementation of protective programs.

5.1 Overview of Sector Protective Programs

The Water Sector's strategy to protect critical infrastructure supports the DHS's risk management framework, SSA Implementation Actions as outlined in the NIPP, and the sector's desire to ensure to the best of its ability the continuity of business.

This includes procedures designed to prevent, detect, respond to, and recover from terrorist attacks, other intentional acts, natural disasters, or other hazards. Such procedures mitigate threats, reduce vulnerability to an attack or other disaster, and minimize consequences, thereby enabling timely and efficient response and restoration after an event.

As mentioned in previous sections, the Water Sector, which is comprised of both drinking water and wastewater assets, has a long history of implementing programs to protect public health and the environment under the SDWA and CWA. In almost all cases, these protective efforts encompass a multi-barrier approach.

Because water is essential for life and the operation of many other sectors, to secure its infrastructure the Water Sector has developed multilayered protective programs. For example, drinking water systems typically rely on a variety of protective programs that include source water protection, treatment and treatment redundancy, monitoring using certified laboratories and appropriately certified operators, and mechanisms to educate the public about water quality and inform them of any violations.

As a result of the completion of vulnerability (risk) assessments by many wastewater utilities and drinking water utilities serving more than 3,300 persons, Water Sector utilities have identified critical components and developed and installed countermeasures to fit their own unique circumstances. Countermeasures range from improving staff awareness and training to enhancing a system's security posture to hardening assets by creating additional redundancies. Equally important for the continuity of business is development of a robust response and recovery capability. Many system components, because of their distributed locations, access by the public, or other reasons do not lend themselves to hardening or cost-effective countermeasures. Preventing or detecting a manmade or naturally occurring event may not always be possible; therefore, improving a system's response and recovery capability helps achieve the sector's endpoint of maintaining continuity of business.

Important to note is that protective programs are interrelated and are designed to strategically address four goals and several objectives, which also encompass EPA's security program pillars of CIP-prevention, detection, response, and recovery. The protective approach that the sector has taken is to enhance capabilities in all of these areas. The sector understands that it may not always be possible to prevent or detect a manmade or naturally occurring event. Initial security efforts such as installing fencing, locks, and access systems focused more on the concepts of prevention and detection and less on response and recovery efforts; however, the logical progression within the sector has been toward more robust response and recovery efforts. As the sector improves its understanding of interdependencies and coordination in response and recovery aspects of protective programs, its resilience will increase, and so will the reduction of consequences, thereby reducing risks.

EPA and its Water Sector security partners have developed holistic and integrated protective programs for all sector assets. EPA has focused on those assets that service high-density population areas (more than 100,000 people). This focus on the Nation's largest utilities is due to the potential for the greatest consequence from an intentional act or natural disaster that would have direct and significant negative impacts on public health and local or regional economies. Sector security partners, working collaboratively, continue to strive to minimize the impediments that a utility owner/operator may face while trying to implement protective program actions. Some of the major challenges that the sector faces in implementing security programs are identified in detail in section 6 of the SSP.

5.1.1 Coordination Within the Sector

Coordination and cooperation are integral in planning and executing CIP activities and programs. EPA consistently coordinates its security efforts with its Water Sector security partners-public/private utilities; the WSCC; GCC; national associations; State, local, and tribal governments; research foundations; and other Federal agencies-to seek input and direction, set priorities, identify gaps, and develop next steps. This coordination is critical to ensure that protective programs are properly evaluated and new efforts are properly developed. It will also ensure that limited resources are allocated and used most efficiently. More information on how coordination in the sector occurs can be found in section 8 of the SSP.

5.1.2 Description of Example Protective Programs

The Water Sector's goals and objectives provide the framework to develop and implement protective programs that are envisioned to realize a more secure and resilient sector against all hazards. EPA programs and sector security partner organizations have all taken action to support the sector's needs.

Owners and operators are responsible for implementing CIP activities at the utility level, which allows protective programs to be tailored to the geography and conditions of that locality, with a focus on the greatest risk (threat, vulnerability, and consequence). Many water and wastewater utilities have conducted risk assessments and spent millions of dollars to reduce identified vulnerabilities and install protective measures. While various security partners may take the lead on any one project identified, collectively the sector is coordinating this work and communicating these activities to minimize duplication of effort, maximizing resources and expertise within the sector and ensuring that the all-hazards concept is being integrated within its security work.

The Water Sector has identified strategic goals for improving its security posture. This section highlights just a few of the many programs within the sector that support its goals. Example programs for each goal are described below.

Goal 1: Sustain protection of public health and the environment:

- *Water Security Initiative*, formerly known as WaterSentinel. In 2005, EPA initiated its Water Security Initiative to pursue appropriate design of a contamination warning system to minimize public health and economic impacts of an attack on the water supply and distribution systems of a drinking water asset. The overall goal of the initiative is to design and demonstrate an effective system for timely detection and response to drinking water contamination threats and incidents through a series of pilot programs that will have broad application to the Nation's drinking water utilities of all sizes. The first Water Security Initiative pilot was initiated in fiscal year (FY) 2006. Efforts in FYs 2007 and 2008 will involve preparing for and deploying additional pilots in select cities; FY 2008-2011 will entail calibrating the contaminant warning systems, conducting thorough evaluations of each pilot's systems, and promoting nationwide adoption of Water Security Initiative-based contamination warning systems through dissemination of guidance and training. Water Sector stakeholders are actively participating in this initiative; a Water Security Initiative Executive Committee has been established to provide stakeholder input to the initiative. This committee is made up of representatives from drinking water utilities; public health agencies; laboratories; first-responders; law enforcement; and Federal, State, and local governments. The initiative is being implemented in three phases to: (1) develop the conceptual design of a system for timely detection and response to drinking water contamination to minimize public health and economic impacts; (2) test and demonstrate a contamination warning system through pilots at drinking water utilities and municipalities, and make refinements to design as needed based upon pilot results; and (3) expand the approach through outreach, training, and practical guidance to promote and support voluntary national adoption of an effective, sustainable contamination warning system. Each participant on the Executive Committee will be asked to provide input and perspectives to EPA as it evaluates the initiative pilot(s) and expands the initiative to voluntary national adoption under implementation phases II and III. EPA considers individual input critical to the long-term success of the initiative. Committee members will provide valuable insight in review of the Water Security Initiative evaluation plan to measure the success of the initial pilot; review the accomplishments and lessons learned from the initial pilot; identify refinements to the design for the purpose of maximizing applicability to utilities of diverse characteristics; review various guidance documents and related materials; identify the opportunities and challenges in voluntary national adoption of the Water Security Initiative model; and identify dual-use and multiple benefits of the initiative. Additional information on contaminant warning system research needs can be found in section 7 of this SSP.

  – **By the end of 2007, EPA will produce and share information with the Water Sector on the lessons learned from its first Water Security Initiative pilot, with a specific focus on contaminant warning systems and consequence management planning.**

- *Water Laboratory Alliance (WLA)*. EPA will fulfill its requirement under HSPD-9 to enhance the security of drinking water utilities through development of a laboratory network that is able to support drinking water monitoring and surveillance programs. EPA will help establish a nationwide network of Federal, State, local government, and commercial laboratories capable of analyzing for standard chemical, biological, and radiological contaminants in drinking water resulting from terrorist attacks, other intentional acts, natural disasters, and other hazards.

- *Fourteen Features of an Active and Effective Security Program*. To further sustain protection of public health and the environment, EPA, in collaboration with its sector security partners, will continue the ongoing promotion, use, and adoption of the features of an active and effective security program in the Water Sector. These features are associated with the four over-arching pillars—prevention, detection, response, and recovery—and are in many cases consistent with the steps needed to maintain technical, managerial, and operational performance capacity related to overall water quality. Many utilities may be able to adopt some of the features with minimal, if any, capital investment. The overarching goal of this project is to increase development and implementation of voluntary active and effective water security programs by increasing awareness of the features and demonstrating the viability of practices identified through case studies. EPA, in collaboration with its security partners, plans to conduct strategic outreach efforts to promote awareness of, and ways to implement, an active and effective water security program. At every stage in the project, EPA will work with its security partners to understand their perspectives and interests, resulting in all partners assisting utilities to adopt the features of high-quality security programs.

- *Security Culture.* Water Sector utilities understand the importance of integrating security into the daily utility culture, and in many cases have set up training and/or new operating procedures for existing staff and new training and procedural checks for hiring new employees. Utilities have also set up more secure procedures for facility visits and deliveries, and removed information from public Web sites about facility location and other information recognized as sensitive in a post-September 11 world.

Goal 2: Recognize and reduce risks in the Water Sector:

- *Risk Assessments.* Drinking water and wastewater utilities performed risk assessments based on several methodologies developed by sector security partners. Risk assessment tools such as the Risk Assessment Methodology: Water, Security and Environmental Management System, and Vulnerability Self-Assessment Tool have all been developed to better reduce risk across the sector. More information on these methodologies can be found in section 3 of this SSP.

- *Incident Reporting and Strategic Sector Assessment.* The Water Sector's informational arm, the WaterISAC, has implemented a reporting mechanism that allows utilities to share incident information in a standardized format. Combined with other information sources, WaterISAC analyses can assess when there may be imminent threats. Furthermore, the Federal Government assists utilities by providing generalized and, when necessary, detailed threat information. The DHS, in collaboration with the CIA, FBI, and EPA, recently released its *Joint Strategic Sector Assessment for Drinking Water and Wastewater Utilities.* This Unclassified/For Official Use Only document identifies generalized threats that the Water Sector needs to consider as it continues to improve its security posture.

- *Consequence Analysis.* EPA, in collaboration with its Water Sector security partners, has initiated a consequence analysis project that, when completed, will help utilities improve their own security programs based on the consequence analysis. More details can be found in section 3 of this SSP.

Goal 3: Maintain a resilient infrastructure:

- *Mutual Aid and Assistance Agreements.* The Water Sector's professional associations, with support from EPA, are working to encourage local utilities in every State to establish intrastate mutual aid agreements such as Water / Wastewater Agency Response Networks (WARNs) to enhance preparedness and improve incident response. Federal, State, and local government agencies are assisting these efforts. To fully implement these ongoing programs, the Water Sector in the near future will: (1) develop outreach materials and facilitate meetings, workshops, trainings, conference calls, Web casts, and other communications; (2) provide administrative support; (3) provide technical support; and (4) assist in formation of new WARNs.

- *Consequence Management Plan (CMP).* When completed in 2007, this guidance will describe the actions utilities could take in response to a contamination or threat warning. The CMP will guide both investigative actions, to help determine the incident's credibility, and response actions, to protect public health and safety and minimize economic impacts. The CMP will also address risk communication issues, both internal to the utility and with the general public, and will outline remediation and recovery actions to restore essential services, decontaminate the water system, and return to normal operations. Utilities will be able to use this guide to improve their own protective programs.

- *Tabletop Exercises and Trainings to Understand Interdependencies.* EPA and the Water Sector associations have developed extensive training programs and tools to help utilities communicate with local first-responders and public health providers about the effects of security incidents on these interdependent infrastructures. Although the trainings and tabletops are not specifically designed to highlight interdependencies, it becomes evident to those outside the Water Sector who participate in trainings and local tabletop exercises their interdependency with water.

- *Commitment to the Partnership Model.* The WSCC and GCC, established under the NIPP's partnership model, were formed in 2004 and 2005, respectively. This ongoing partnership will continue to improve communication and outreach across the sector.

- *WaterISAC.* Established in 2002, the WaterISAC and its free service, WaterSC, have been designated by the Water Sector as its primary mechanism for effectively and efficiently sharing security-related information. This service, managed by AMWA, was designed by the sector to provide America's drinking water and wastewater utilities with a highly secure Web-based environment for warning, informing, and responding to an array of all-hazard incidents and events, including physical attack, contamination, cyber threats, and natural disasters. The majority of State drinking water primacy agencies are sub-scribers to the WaterISAC, thus providing a mechanism to reach small and medium drinking water utilities.

- *Communication with Local Utilities.* To have access to security tools developed by EPA, associations, or other organizations, many local utilities belong to one or more of the Water Sector's associations, WaterISAC, or receive assistance from State agencies or technical assistance providers. The associations have extensive procedures for sharing information. In addition, utilities can access most of EPA's tools and guidance documents for security directly on the Agency's Web site.

EPA will continue to coordinate with its Water Sector security partners to eliminate gaps and identify vulnerabilities. Implementing the sector's vision, goals, and objectives will require coordination with all partners, especially when evaluating or developing existing and new protective programs. These collaborative efforts help utilities be better prepared to prevent, detect, respond to, and recover from terrorist attacks, other intentional acts, natural disasters, and other hazards, thereby better protecting the Nation's critical water infrastructure.

5.2 Determining Protective Program Needs

Prior to September 11, EPA established a dialogue and working group comprised of Water Sector security partners and orga-nizations to discuss security needs related to PDD-63. Soon after September 11, and with passage of the Bioterrorism Act, this working group became instrumental in helping EPA identify protective program needs and gaps. These needs were identified through regular and ongoing interaction with security partners, by holding meetings and workshops with security partners, and through exchanges with the DHS, law enforcement, and other Federal agencies to gain a better understanding of the vulnerabilities, threats, and consequences in the Water Sector. Collectively, all the security partners helped to define protective programs designed to prevent, detect, respond to, and recover from terrorist attacks, other intentional acts, natural disasters, and other hazards.

In September 2002, EPA created the NHSRC to manage, coordinate, and support a variety of security-related R&D efforts. To manage the planning and conduct of its R&D activities in water security, EPA, in coordination with its Water Sector security partners, created a process that resulted in development of the Water Security Research and Technical Support Action Plan (referred to as the Research Action Plan). The process is adaptable to the needs of the Water Sector, and will be used as the basis for EPA's annual updates of the DHS's National Critical Infrastructure Protection (NCIP) Research and Development Plan. Since development of the Research Action Plan, EPA and its partners have held numerous workshops and symposia, with research organizations such as WERF and AwwaRF participating. These activities helped to identify research-related needs and gaps and obtain input and direction on development of Water Sector security programs. Additional information on sector security R&D activities is provided in section 7 of the SSP.

In addition to Water Sector security partner input, security "needs analyses" have been undertaken by entities such as the Government Accountability Office (GAO), which has written three different reports that pertain to Water Sector security.

These reports include Drinking Water: Experts' Views on How Future Federal Spending Can Best Be Spent to Improve Security, issued in October 2003; Wastewater: Experts' Views on How Future Federal Spending Can Best Be Spent to Improve Security, issued in March 2005; and Securing Wastewater Facilities: Utilities Have Made Important Upgrades but Further Improvements to Key System Components May Be Limited by Costs and Other Constraints, issued in March 2006.

EPA will continue to take a number of approaches to identify protective program needs in the Water Sector, the most important being regular communication with its sector security partners and the DHS, as well as other Federal agencies. This ensures that EPA is meeting the needs of its security partners at the local, State, and Federal levels, and that tools and protective programs are properly integrated into applicable Federal programs, most importantly into day-to-day utility operations. EPA, other government agencies, and private organizations are pursuing many initiatives jointly. The collaborative nature of EPA's current research increases the likelihood that initiatives with the greatest potential are being pursued. As stated previously, EPA will continue to coordinate with its security partners to seek input and direction, and to identify gaps and next steps. Furthermore, the Agency continues to promote adoption of active and effective security programs by utilities which encompass the implementation and protective actions a Water-Sector utility should consider when working to better protect critical infrastructure from manmade or naturally occurring events. Coordination among security partners is critical to ensure that protective programs are properly evaluated and new efforts are properly developed.

5.3 Protective Program Implementation

With the exception of requirements in the Bioterrorism Act, implementation and maintenance of protective programs in the Water Sector is voluntary and generally occurs at the local, utility (asset) level. EPA has encouraged implementation of protective programs by working with its security partners to develop useful tools, training, technical assistance, guidance, and outreach and communication mechanisms that provide assistance to Water Sector assets to enhance their security posture.

As mentioned previously, most asset owner/operators in the Water Sector have protective programs in place to address the goals identified in section 1 of the SSP. Each program is unique depending on local conditions and the risks to a particular asset. EPA, in collaboration with the Water Sector, is engaged with the DHS and other Federal agencies in implementation of protective programs for Water and the other 16 CI/KR sectors. For example, the DHS's National Cyber Security Division (NCSD), WERF, and AwwaRF are creating a tool that allows utilities to better identify SCADA vulnerabilities. Furthermore, as Water and other critical infrastructure sectors continue to identify dependencies and interdependencies, SSAs will work together to implement protective actions that help mitigate vulnerable dependencies/interdependencies and better prepare assets to prevent, detect, respond to, and recover from terrorist attacks, other intentional acts, natural disasters, and other hazards. A more detailed discussion of dependent/interdependent critical infrastructures is provided in section 3 of the SSP and further details on coordination with the sector can be found above and in section 8. Numerous products and tools developed by EPA that incorporate the elements of Water Sector protective programs are already underway and implemented throughout the sector. More details on these products and tools that support protective programs are described in appendix 3.

Most drinking water and wastewater programs are delegated to the States. Therefore, EPA depends heavily on State drinking water primacy agencies and the wastewater permitting authorities, which implement the SDWA and CWA. EPA is providing counterterrorism grants to States and Territories to support coordination and communication activities at drinking water utilities. States and Territories are encouraged to use these grants for mutual aid, risk assessment, and emergency response planning activities and strategies that will assist Water Sector utilities to implement security enhancements and improve the readiness of individuals and groups involved in first response.

To ensure this coordination, EPA has engaged State organizations such as the ASDWA and ASIWPCA to identify their security concerns. State critical infrastructure-related agencies are particularly concerned with programs related to protection of, interdependencies among, and sharing of information with other critical sectors because of their direct service to all citizens.

5.4 Protective Program Performance

Every time a protective program is implemented, the security posture for both the individual asset where the protective measure is implemented and the Water Sector changes. For subsequent protective decisions to be the most cost effective, the security posture of the asset affected needs to be reviewed and updated accordingly to meet the CIP goals and objectives outlined in section 1. In developing new projects and evaluating current projects, EPA in collaboration with its security partners needs to explicitly confront the issue of whether the sector's work addresses the most pressing security needs of the sector. The sector meets high-priority security needs by implementing protective programs that consider prevention, detection, response, and recovery as they relate to vulnerabilities and consequences from, and the threat of, terrorists attacks, other intentional acts, natural disasters, and other hazards that might impact the Water Sector.

The sector's protective program approach relies on performance management and program evaluation that make explicit the underlying assumptions about how the protective programs are supposed to work, recognize the fluidity of protective programs, and allow for changing circumstances. The sector continues to build a shared understanding of its protective programs among all relevant security partners. Measuring success by providing a transparent evaluation framework for tracking progress promotes effective communication about the security program and places emphasis on the shared responsibility among various parties in achieving desired outcomes. This process sets the direction for development of measures of success to meet security performance reporting needs. Section 6 of the SSP discusses how EPA is working with its Water Sector security partners to identify the process to measure security progress (performance) in achieving the sector's CIP vision and goals.

6. Measure Progress

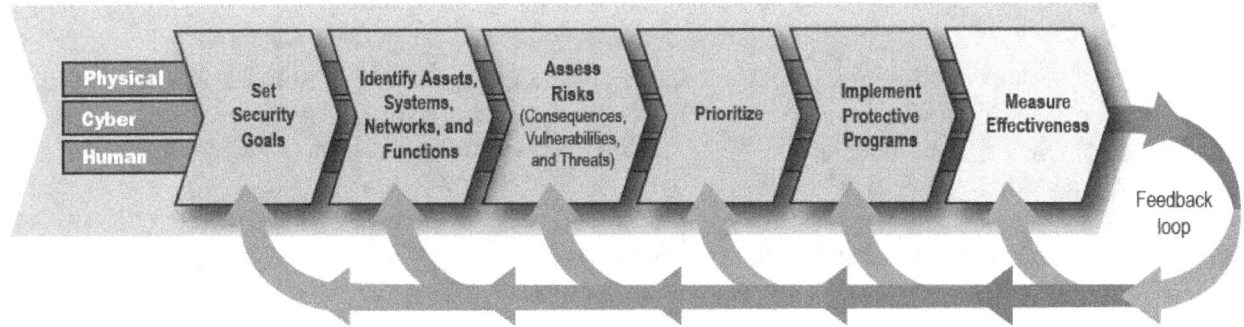

Continuous improvement to enhance protection of CI/KR

Measuring progress is part of the NIPP risk management framework. While the DHS focuses on measuring progress across all CI/KR sectors using core metrics, EPA is responsible for measuring it in the Water Sector using additional sector-specific metrics. This section of the SSP describes how EPA and its Water Sector security partners will interact to develop sector-specific metrics, and how the sector plans to voluntarily collect, verify, and report data as requested in the NIPP on core metrics as well as the sector-specific metrics. These metrics will be used to measure security progress and support continuous improvement in the sector.

6.1 CI/KR Performance Measurement

The performance of Water Sector protective activities and programs and the actual risk reduction achieved within the sector and across all CI/KR sectors will be measured using a standard set of core metrics developed by the DHS and a set of sector-specific metrics developed by each sector. These metrics will be used as a basis to establish accountability, document actual performance, facilitate evaluation, and promote effective management. To be effective, the NIPP performance measurement program will work with cooperation and collaboration from EPA and owner/operators in reporting on core metrics and developing and reporting on sector-specific metrics.

The NIPP strategy uses a metrics-based system of performance evaluation to constantly improve the alignment of protective programs to the dynamic threat environment and to drive increased awareness of the threat environment across critical infrastructure owner/operators. These metrics will measure program accomplishments and drive continuous improvement of CIP activities. The NIPP strategy includes three types of quantitative indicators to measure program effectiveness:

- **Descriptive metrics** characterize the sector, such as how many assets of a particular type are in the sector. Descriptive metrics are necessary to understand sector resources and activities; however, they do not reflect CIP performance.

- **Process (output) metrics** measure whether specific activities that are important to a program's execution were performed as planned, track the progression of a task, or report on the output of a process, such as inventorying assets. This includes, for example, the number of systems that did vulnerability assessments in a given year.

- **Outcome metrics** track progress toward a strategic goal in terms of beneficial results rather than level of activity. An example is the change in the number of facilities assessed as high risk following implementation of protective actions.

6.1.1 Metrics

The metrics outlined in the NIPP are divided into two groups: (1) core metrics and (2) sector-specific metrics. Core metrics are basic measures that can be tracked across each sector to enable comparison and analysis among different types of CI/KR. Sector-specific metrics will be tailored to the unique characteristics of the sector and will help monitor security progress.

6.1.1.1 Core CIP Metrics

The core CIP metrics, which will be common across all sectors, will be a set of descriptive, process, and outcome metrics that measure progress made by and across all CI/KR sectors to implement the NIPP risk management framework. These metrics will be developed by the DHS in conjunction with the 17 SSAs and other security partners, which include the SCCs and GCCs. When these core metrics are finalized, the DHS plans to work with EPA and the WSCC and GCC to identify the most effective and cost-efficient way to collect responses to submit on behalf of the Water Sector. Core metrics will be assessed on an ongoing basis, with summary reports compiled regularly (likely semiannually).

6.1.1.2 Sector-Specific Metrics

EPA is working with its Water Sector security partners to develop sector-specific metrics to more thoroughly evaluate progress made by the sector toward the goals and objectives set forth by the NIPP and Water SSP. A CIPAC will be jointly formed by the Water Sector and GCCs to examine, evaluate, and select appropriate metrics to assess the sector's security progress. The metrics that are developed will be based on the goals, objectives, and supporting strategies outlined in section 1 of this SSP. The CIPAC will also evaluate reporting and verification options. EPA has led a number of iterative steps, discussed below, to evaluate potential sector metrics. The product of EPA's efforts will serve to inform the CIPAC Joint Working Group.

National Drinking Water Advisory Council's Water Security Working Group

In 2004, EPA commissioned formation of a National Drinking Water Advisory Council Water Security Working Group (NDWAC WSWG) to start looking into developing Water Sector security measures. The working group's composition of 16 members was diverse, representing drinking water and wastewater utilities of all sizes (small, medium, and large), public health agencies, States, and environmental and rate-setting organizations. The group's charge was to provide recommendations that: (1) identify, compile, and characterize voluntary features of an active and effective security program for drinking water and wastewater utilities, and provide an approach for considering and adopting these features at the utility level; (2) consider mechanisms to provide recognition and incentives that facilitate a broad and receptive response by the Water Sector to implement these features, and to make recommendations as appropriate; and (3) consider mechanisms to measure the extent of implementation of these features, identify impediments to their implementation, and make recommendations as appropriate.

In June 2005, the full NDWAC made final recommendations to EPA for mechanisms to measure and track the Water Sector's security progress. While described here, the measures were developed prior to the sector developing goals and objectives and without full consideration of an all-hazards approach. NDWAC proposed three measures of national water security progress:

1. Implementation of "active and effective" security programs as measured by the degree of implementation of the program features and corresponding feature-specific measures;

2. Reduction in security risks as measured by the total number of assets determined to be high security risks and the number of formerly high-risk assets lowered to medium or low risk based on vulnerability assessments; and

3. Reduction in the inherent risk of utility operations as measured by the Clean Air Act's section 112(r), on hazardous substance reporting, and by the number of utilities that convert from gaseous chlorine to other forms of chlorine or other treatment methods.

In deliberations about measures, the NDWAC WSWG was guided by the following key concepts:

- Measures must help individual utilities to better understand their own performance relative to the features of active and effective security programs;

- Simple, binary (e.g., yes/no) measures focused on activities may be appropriate at some utilities; over time, utilities should strive for measures of program achievement, outcomes, and performance;

- Strict comparability across utilities is not supportable for all measures at this time;

- Clear security policies, plans, and priorities are important precursors to effective measurement;

- Who will measure, who will use the measure, and how it will be used are important to acceptance of the measure by utilities, and to the ability of customers and the public to trust measurement results;

- A measure's baseline should not penalize proactive organizations; and

- Developing and tracking a measure should not compromise security.

Measures Testing Group

As follow-up to NDWAC's recommendations on national measures for water security, EPA formed the Measures Testing Group (MTG) for National Aggregate Measures of Water Security in January 2006. The MTG is comprised of representatives from small, medium, and large drinking water and wastewater utilities and from State primacy agencies. EPA solicited nominations for membership from the Water Sector. The emphasis in selecting the MTG membership was to identify actual utility owners, operators, and managers who would be tasked with ultimately implementing any measurement system.

The primary purpose of creating the MTG was to evaluate the strengths and weaknesses of the metric recommendations made by NDWAC. As of November 2006, the MTG plans to report its findings to EPA by the end of 2006. These will not be recommendations but rather a non-prioritized list of options. The report will include discussion of additional options for reporting on national water security progress that were not outlined by NDWAC. Upon reporting its findings, the MTG will have fulfilled its task and will disband.

CIPAC Joint Working Group

At the beginning of 2007, EPA plans to convene with the WSCC and GCC in a CIPAC Joint Working Group to review the findings prepared by the MTG and decide on the elements of a final performance measurement system.

Alignment of Sector-Specific Metrics With Water Sector Goals and Objectives

EPA's initial efforts with the NDWAC WSWG and MTG, which were initiated prior to development of the goals and objectives of the Water Sector as described in section 1 of the SSP, will need to be aligned. Considering the challenges to data collection, information sensitivity, and other limitations, EPA and the CIPAC Working Group will seek to finalize a framework for assessing the sector's progress in meeting its goals.

6.1.2 Information Collection and Verification

Although identifying potential measures of progress is possible, a discussion on information collection and verification is critical to ensure that measures are meaningful and reflect the goals and security posture of the sector, and that the data can be collected, verified, and reported. In deliberations on measures and reporting, the participants in both the NDWAC WSWG and MTG agreed that:

- Participation in a national measurement program should be voluntary; and

- Results of national aggregate measures should be presented only in aggregated form, and issues associated with the need for data confidentiality should be resolved before any national measurement program is put in place.

Though the groups determined that a purely voluntary effort may face challenges of providing a complete and accurate picture of sector progress, they also identified factors that could prompt utilities to participate in a voluntary national aggregate measurement effort. These include:

- Credible, voluntary measurement efforts will increase the overall credibility of the sector; and

- A defined measurement effort to evaluate security needs and progress will build national support for security efforts and funding by demonstrating need.

Protection of individual utility-level data was also recognized as a critical issue, and will be the key element in determining whether utilities participate in such a reporting program.

6.1.3 Reporting

HSPD-7 requires SSAs to provide the Secretary of Homeland Security with annual reports that serve as a primary tool for assessing performance and reporting on progress in the sector. The Sector Annual Report developed by each SSA should:

- Provide a common vehicle across all sectors to communicate CI/KR protection performance and progress to security partners and other government entities;

- Establish a baseline of existing sector-specific CI/KR protection programs and initiatives;

- Identify plans for SSA resource requirements and the departmental CI/KR protection budget;

- Determine and explain how sector efforts support the national effort;

- Provide an overall progress report for a given sector and measure that progress against the national CI/KR protection goals for that sector;

- Provide feedback to the DHS, sectors, and other government entities that will be used as the basis for continuous improvement of the CI/KR protection program; and

- Help identify and share successful practices from successful programs.

EPA submitted the Water Sector CI/KR 2006 Annual Report to DHS in July 2006. In this report, EPA outlined the sector's vision statement and the four overarching goals recently developed by the sector through the SSP process. The report also addressed coordination efforts, priorities, R&D efforts, funding progress, and gaps.

As the Water Sector is currently in the process of developing sector-specific metrics and reporting measures, it is premature for EPA to report on anything other than perhaps some basic descriptive core metrics. Note that the NIPP and its component SSPs include a process for annual review; periodic interim updates as required; and will be reissued every three years, or more frequently, if directed by the Secretary of Homeland Security. The NIPP and SSP revision processes will include developing or updating any documents necessary to carry out security-related activities such as progress in the development of water-sector-related measures.

As sector-specific metrics are finalized, EPA will work with the GCC and WSCC to identify: (1) the parties responsible and the format for reporting results; (2) how metrics data will be reported to the DHS; (3) how the NIPP reporting process aligns with

EPA's reporting responsibilities; and (4) whether the metric information collected will be shared with the sector at large or the public, and to the extent in which it is shared, if at all, the process for sharing such information.

6.2 Implementation Actions (Initiatives and Milestones) and Challenges

Under the NIPP, the DHS has identified a series of implementation actions that is to be completed as the Water SSP is applied over the next few years. These actions, shown in table 6-1, represent the major actions that the DHS, EPA and/or the Water Sector will undertake to achieve a secure and resilient infrastructure. Completion of these actions depends on the availability of resources. The sector expects to leverage existing capabilities and activities to pursue multiyear efforts to meet national protection needs; many of these actions are ongoing efforts, without target end dates. Efforts will build on existing work in government agencies as well as public and private sector security partners.

In the implementation action matrix below, only those security partners with primary responsibility for a given task are identified; however, virtually all security partners have at least a supporting role in every action listed. It should be recognized that all of the listed actions and timelines associated with their completion are not mandatory, and participation by sector owner/operators and security partners is voluntary.

These matrix implementation actions are broken out by their associated NIPP sections and are specifically identified in appendix 2B of the NIPP. These voluntary actions included in the matrix are the shared responsibilities of many Water Sector security partners, EPA, and the DHS. Primary responsibility for each implementation action has been identified in the matrix as well as supporting roles. Most of these voluntary actions will be led by EPA or the DHS; milestones are specified in terms of the number of days after the June 30, 2006, the release date of the NIPP. When taking into consideration the timelines set in the implementation action matrix below, note that the dates identified in the matrix are only targets; most of these actions are ongoing and remain fluid. Therefore, these dates are cited only as an estimate for completion and are not firm deadlines. While EPA and its sector security partners will strive to meet the timeframes set in the matrix below, the suggestion of the dates does not hold any organization to a deadline.

Table 6-1: Implementation Action Matrix

Notes:

X = Primary responsibility   O = Support responsibility (may be required to qualify for grants)

+ = Milestone indicator   ✓ = Milestone Completed   NLT = Not later than

NIPP Sections	Implementation Actions	Milestone				Security Partner					
		NLT 90 Days After SSP Approval	NLT 180 Days	NLT 365 Days	Target-Specific Date	DHS	SSA	Other Federal	State or Territory	Local and Tribal	Public/Private Sector
2	**Authorities, Roles, and Responsibilities**										
	Review NIPP and establish processes needed to support NIPP implementation	+ ✓			09/30/2006	X	X	X	X	X	X
	Incorporate NIPP into strategies for cooperation with foreign countries and international/ multinational organizations		+		12/31/2006	X	X	X	O	O	O
3	**The Protection Program Strategy: Managing Risk**										
	Develop sector-specific CI/KR inventory guidance		+		12/31/2006	X	X	O	O	O	O
	Review existing risk assessment methodologies to determine compatibility with NIPP baseline criteria		+		12/31/2006	X	X	X	X	X	X
	Establish timeline for: (1) development of sector-specific risk methodologies and (2) conducting consequence-based top screening for all CI/KR sectors		+		12/31/2006	X	X	O	O	O	O
	Conduct and validate consequence assessments of priority CI/KR as identified by the top-screening process			+	06/30/2006	X	X	X	X	X	X
	Conduct or facilitate vulnerability assessments in priority CI/KR sectors and identify cross-sector vulnerabilities			+	06/30/2006	X	X	X	X	X	X

NIPP Sections	Implementation Actions	Milestone				Security Partner					
		NLT 90 Days After SSP Approval	NLT 180 Days	NLT 365 Days	Target-Specific Date	DHS	SSA	Other Federal	State or Territory	Local and Tribal	Public/Private Sector
	Develop sector-specific CI/KR threat assessments needed to support comprehensive risk assessments	+ ✓			09/30/2006	X	O	O	O	O	O
	Provide guidance on metrics for annual reporting and national, cross-sector comparative analysis	+ ✓			09/30/2006	X	O	O	O	O	O
4	**Organizing and Partnering for CI/KR Protection**										
	Establish all SCCs, GCCs, and SLTGCC in accordance with NIPP partnership model	+ ✓			09/30/2006	X	X	O	O	O	X
	Complete rollout of HSIN; implement policies for vetting and disseminating information to security partners			+	06/30/2007	X	X	O	O	O	O
	Identify sector-level information-sharing mechanisms and ensure information protection practices comply with guidance for protection of classified or sensitive information. Publish PCII final rule	+ ✓			09/30/2006	X	X	O	O	O	O
	Develop Annual CI/KR Protection Information Requirements Report		+		12/31/2006	X	O	O	O	O	O
	Work with DOS to review charter and coordinating mechanisms for the IWG that coordinates U.S. international CI/KR protection outreach and update to align with NIPP	+			09/30/2006	X	X	X	O	O	O
5	**Integrating CI/KR Protection as Part of the Homeland Security Mission**										
	Coordinate SSP development in collaboration with security partners and submit to the DHS with appropriate documentation of concurrence		+		12/31/2006	O	X	X	X	X	X

NIPP Sections	Implementation Actions	Milestone				Security Partner					
		NLT 90 Days After SSP Approval	NLT 180 Days	NLT 365 Days	Target-Specific Date	DHS	SSA	Other Federal	State or Territory	Local and Tribal	Public/Private Sector
	Review and revise CI/KR-related plans as needed to reinforce linkage between NIPP steady-state CI/KR protection and NRP incident management requirements		+		12/31/2006	X	X	X	X	X	X
	Review current CI/KR protection measures to ensure alignment with HSAS threat conditions and specific threat vectors/scenarios		+		12/31/2006	X	X	X	X	X	X
6	**Ensuring an Effective, Efficient Program Over the Long Term**										
	Develop and implement comprehensive national CI/KR protection awareness program		+		12/31/2006	X	X	O	O	O	O
	Review and revise training programs to ensure consistency with NIPP requirements		+		12/31/2006	X	X	X	X	X	X
	Provide initial NIPP training to security partners	+			09/30/2006	X	X	O	O	O	O
	Ensure national exercises include CI/KR protection and interaction between NIPP, NRP	+			09/30/2006	X	X	O	O	O	O
	Communicate requirements for CI/KR-related R&D to the DHS for use in national R&D planning effort				7/1 (Annual)	O	X	X	O	O	O
	Identify all databases, data services and sources, and modeling capabilities with CI/KR application		+		12/31/2006	X	X	X	X	X	X
	Conduct first annual review of NIPP and SSPs			+	06/30/2007	X	X	X	X	X	X

NIPP Sections	Implementation Actions	Milestone				Security Partner					
		NLT 90 Days After SSP Approval	NLT 180 Days	NLT 365 Days	Target-Specific Date	DHS	SSA	Other Federal	State or Territory	Local and Tribal	Public/Private Sector
7	**Providing Resources for the CI/KR Protection Program**										
	Submit Sector CI/KR Protection Annual Report to DHS				7/1 (Annual)	O	X	O	O	O	O
	Submit National CI/KR Protection Annual Report to Executive Office of the President				Sep 1 (Annual)	X	O	O	O	O	O
	Review homeland security grant guidance to ensure requirements are consistent with NIPP	+ ✓			09/30/2006	X	O	O	O	O	O
	Advise State, local, and tribal governments of SSA grant programs and/or other sources that can support NIPP		+		12/31/2006	X	X	O	O	O	O
	Apply for homeland security grants to address CI/KR protection efforts per DHS/G&T guidance				*	O	O	O	X	X	O

* Required application deadlines are specified within individual program guidance and may change annually. Dates for submitting grant applications, program requirements, and other required reports to the DHS will be specified in annual grant program guidance and application kits. The States will work with local and tribal jurisdictions to ensure compliance with all other related reporting requirements.

The Water Sector continues to encounter hurdles in its CIP efforts, such as those actions identified in the implementation action matrix above. Metric-related challenges will be addressed in section 6.3 below; this section of the SSP focuses on some of the major non-metric-related barriers facing the sector. These challenges are as follows:

1. The importance of day-to-day O&M; infrastructure repair; and regulatory costs for protection of public health and the environment by utility owner/operators cannot be overemphasized. However, these costs do compete with the level of funding and effort an individual utility can invest in security enhancements. Furthermore, owner/operators have difficulty getting official budget endorsement and approval for needed security enhancements without revealing asset vulnerabilities. The job of all sector security partners is to identify the mutual benefits a utility can gain by taking security into consideration when addressing other priorities.

2. The DHS identifies "consequence" as the impact of an attack on public health, the economy, national psyche, and governance abilities. However, for consequence analysis to be acceptable, it must address, at least minimally, the quantitative measures of both the public health and economic impacts of an attack, and not the qualitative measures of psychological

and governance matters. EPA has taken steps towards identifying attack consequences by applying the CARVER + Shock methodology to identify the public health and economic impacts; however, this analysis is limited to the potential impacts of contamination on a drinking water distribution system and does not consider the compounding or independent impacts of a physical or cyber attack. Further consequence analysis work is being initiated by EPA in coordination with its sector security partners; the challenge here is that full assessment of consequences has not been completed. The information resulting from these analyses will assist utility owner/operators to fully identify the public health and economic impacts of other scenarios on both drinking water and wastewater utilities, thereby making their risk assessments more robust and informative. The consequence analysis results will also allow owner/operators to make more informed decisions on security enhancements and subsequent resource allocation.

3. The Water Sector shares a number of vital dependencies and interdependencies with other CI/KR. While progress is being made to identify these relationships, work is still needed to address implementation steps to create cross-sector protective programs. With the DHS taking the lead, the sector will help enhance existing coordination mechanisms among all stakeholders. This coordination is crucial and may require development of new interpersonal relationships and more regular and effective communication mechanisms to further understand and address cross-sector dependencies/interdependencies.

4. Information sharing and communications are vital to CIP activities. The WaterISAC was established as a resource for the Water Sector to gather, analyze, and disseminate threat information that is specific to the sector. The WaterISAC offers service to the entire sector and is in the process of incorporating the Homeland Security Information Network (HSIN) into its operations. Since not all utilities are WaterISAC subscribers, the sector and EPA must continue to encourage drinking water and wastewater utilities to become subscribers or sign up to receive WaterSC basic free information.

6.3 Metrics Challenges and Continuous Improvement

Water Sector security partners assist to minimize the challenges utility owner/operators may face while trying to implement protective program actions. EPA and its security partners adapt CIP efforts to account for security progress achieved and ever-changing threats, vulnerabilities, and consequences in the sector. At the national level, metrics will be used to focus Federal and security partners' attention on areas of CIP that warrant additional resources or other changes. The challenges outlined above in section 6.2 may indirectly impact measurement of progress and overall implementation of protective actions. This section of the SSP focuses on the foremost challenges, both current and future, of measuring progress in the sector.

There is the recognition that a significant number of drinking water and wastewater utilities not impacted by the Bioterrorism Act have voluntarily taken steps to assess their risks and develop or update ERPs. As traditional stewards of public health and the environment, utility owner/operators have been very proactive in incorporating security and emergency preparedness initiatives into their operating protocols to establish greater infrastructure resiliency. A sound balance between the need to keep vulnerability and risk information secure while ensuring that these assessments are actually performed has been achieved by the Bioterrorism Act.

The vulnerabilities, event consequences, and capabilities of typical small utilities are substantially different than larger utilities. Provided a small utility is not serving a critical facility, the tools and metrics it uses will of necessity be simpler, less resource intensive, and consistent with the lower likelihood that it will be a target of terrorist attack. However, small facilities that have higher exposures to natural disasters (e.g. coastal utilities or those in hurricane zones) may need somewhat more elaborate response and recovery plans. The most effective measures for small systems will be evaluated through the CIPAC process and will rely heavily on the vulnerability assessment and ERP tool used by the majority of small systems.

Protective program implementation actions in the Water Sector are not mandatory; still, many utilities have performed risk assessments and spent significant time, money, and effort improving their security posture. Obstacles still remain around collection, verification, validation, storage, protection, and tracking of sector security information and measurements.

Utility owner/operators lack confidence that their asset vulnerability and consequence data can be protected by the Federal Government. Furthermore, provisions of the Paperwork Reduction Act (PRA) will impact data collection efforts by Federal agencies.

To provide and protect information that pertains to the Water Sector's security status and to measure security progress, as envisioned under the NIPP, the sector must identify appropriate mechanisms for providing consequence analysis, vulnerability, and threat information to utilities, and needs to develop a mechanism for collecting, verifying, validating, storing, protecting, and tracking sector priorities and critical infrastructure information to illustrate and measure security progress. Working with the DHS's PCII Program, EPA and its security partners need to examine mechanisms to receive voluntarily submitted security data.

EPA will continue to coordinate with all sector security partners to identify and address current as well as future challenges. Implementing the sector's vision, goals, objectives, and milestones will require coordination with all partners when evaluating existing or developing new protective programs and measures of success. These collaborative efforts will, however, help utilities be better prepared for the all-hazards approach, to prevent, detect, respond to, and recover from terrorist attacks, other intentional acts, natural disasters, and other hazards; thereby better protecting the Nation's critical Water Sector infrastructure.

7. CI/KR Protection R&D

7.1 Introduction

The Water Sector has had a long history of investing in R&D initiatives to assist in setting public health standards and emergency response planning. Historically, EPA's R&D efforts have focused on identifying contaminants of concern (chemical, biological, and radiological) and research for setting public health protective standards and protecting the environment. Research into cost-effective treatment technologies and alternative provision of safe drinking water has also been emphasized. EPA along with organizations such as AwwaRF and WERF, have created a robust research agenda to promote safety and security of utilities. However, as the sector developed its research agenda prior to developing its goals and objectives, as outlined in section 1 of this document, it might need to modify the agenda to make it more comprehensive and reflective of its enhanced approach to security. It should be noted that AwwaRF and WERF have contributed significantly to improved utility operations and maintenance research as well as increased knowledge of treatment technologies and approaches.

EPA and its security partners have expanded the Water Sector's historical R&D programs to include research on contaminants that can be weaponized; cleanup and restoration of utilities; new tools and technology to enhance security; and emergency response procedures, including communication with the public and provision of alternative water supplies. R&D initiatives are being conducted by educational institutions, national research laboratories, public and private research foundations, and the Federal Government, among other organizations. This section of the SSP will focus mainly on R&D initiatives being conducted by EPA's NHSRC, and the coordination and collaboration the NHSRC engages in with R&D stakeholders to help assist water-sector utilities be better prepared to prevent, detect, respond to, and recover from terrorist attacks, other intentional acts, natural disasters, and other hazards (all-hazards approach). The section will also describe the management process for implementing and maintaining research activities and aligning the sector's vision and goals with the nine themes and three strategic goals outlined in the DHS's NCIP R&D Plan.

7.2 Overview of Sector R&D

As noted above, the Water Sector has a long history of investing in R&D programs to benefit public health and the environment. Prior to September 11, the sector was already at work developing comprehensive vulnerability (risk) assessment methodologies and expanding its research agenda to meet needs identified in PDD-63 and new security-related threats. The DHS, coordinating with the White House Office of Science and Technology Policy (OSTP), has developed the NCIP R&D Plan. To understand the relationship between EPA's sector security R&D initiatives and the NCIP R&D Plan, it is important to understand that the plan is based on three strategic goals: (1) a national common operating picture for critical infrastructures; (2) a next-generation Internet architecture with security "designed-in" and inherent in all elements rather than added after the fact; and (3) resilient, self-diagnosing, self-healing physical and cyber infrastructure systems. Also important to note is that the

NCIP R&D Plan is divided into nine research-related themes: (1) detection and sensor systems; (2) protection and prevention; (3) entry portals and access portals; (4) insider threats; (5) analysis and decision support methods; (6) response, recovery, and reconstitution; (7) new and emerging threats and vulnerabilities; (8) advanced infrastructure architectures and system designs; and (9) human and social issues. Each of these themes includes physical and cyber R&D, and supports the three NCIP R&D strategic goals, as well as the Water Sector's vision and goals.

EPA's NHSRC manages, coordinates, and supports a variety of research and technical assistance efforts. These efforts are designed to provide appropriate, affordable, effective, and validated technologies and methods for addressing risks posed by chemical, biological, and radiological terror attacks; research focuses on enhancing our ability to detect, contain, and clean up such attacks. NHSRC provides a management structure that ensures effective design and oversight of research and facilitates interaction with EPA program offices and regions, other Federal agencies, the private sector, and research partners. NHSRC's team of scientists and engineers are dedicated to understanding the terrorist threat, communicating the risks, and mitigating the results of attacks. EPA's Office of Research and Development has longstanding relationships with many sector security partners. Many of the R&D projects initiated before September 11 support current and ongoing security-related R&D initiatives. To manage the planning and conduct of R&D activities, EPA coordinated with its security partners to initiate a process that resulted in the Water Security Research and Technical Support Action Plan (Research Action Plan). The Research Action Plan was developed prior to creation of the DHS's NCIP R&D Plan, but activities outlined in it do address the latter plan's themes and strategic goals. Furthermore, the four overarching Water Sector security goals—sustain protection of public health and the environment; recognize and reduce risks in the sector; maintain a resilient infrastructure; and increase communication, outreach, and public confidence—support the Research Action Plan and the NCIP R&D Plan's themes and strategic goals. All of the coordinated activities continue to help utilities be better prepared to prevent, detect, respond to, and recover from terrorist attacks, other intentional acts, natural disasters, and other hazards.

The process that created EPA's Research Action Plan is adaptable to the needs of the Water Sector and is notable for including a wide range of participants who discussed EPA's security research priorities at a series of meetings. In addition to EPA staff, attendees of these meetings included representatives of utilities; professional and industry associations; national laboratories; public advocacy groups; State water programs; water research organizations; vendors and contractors; BuRec, CDC, the DHS, FDA, USACE, USGS, and other Federal agencies such as the National Institute of Occupational Safety and Health, National Institute of Standards and Technology, and National Science Foundation. EPA proposes to use this process as the basis for its annual updates of the National CIP (NCIP) R&D Plan. The Agency also worked with WERF to identify needs and develop projects to improve wastewater security. WERF entered into a cooperative agreement with the Agency to address wastewater security-related activities. To advance this project further, WERF conducted a stakeholder wastewater security symposium. The needs and projects identified at the symposium are reflected in the Research Action Plan.

In recent years, and as described above, EPA has used an extensive, collaborative process to identify water-security research and technology needs. After these needs were identified, a meeting of Federal partners and water utility representatives was convened to evaluate the needs. Input from this meeting resulted in a draft Research Action Plan. In developing and implementing this plan, EPA made a point to engage engineering and technology organizations and sector security partners; public health organizations and other public health stakeholders; and emergency and remedial response organizations and other response stakeholders. In the future, EPA will engage the Water Sector on research priorities through the WSCC and GCC.

To create a robust water security R&D program, EPA met with the National Academy of Sciences (NAS) to obtain an independent peer panel's assessment of its Research Action Plan. The panel transmitted comments to EPA; these comments were reviewed by EPA and, where applicable, were incorporated into the final draft Research Action Plan. NAS then conducted a second review of the draft plan. This review, along with additional input from our security partners from the cosponsored EPA and WEF water security workshops, resulted in the Research Action Plan being updated and finalized in 2005. Additional information on the EPA and WEF water security workshops can be found in appendix 3 of this SSP. As security advancements are made in the Water Sector, CIP R&D efforts will necessitate adaptability, resulting in the need for the Research Action Plan to be updated.

7.3 Sector R&D Requirements and Sector R&D Plan

Now that the NCIP R&D Plan is available, EPA will correlate its existing initiatives with the nine themes and three strategic goals as described in the plan. However, it is premature in this version of the SSP to sort EPA's initiatives according to these themes and goals, as not all of EPA's initiatives may fit into the plan framework and may need to be updated, as already stated in this section.

With regard to indicating those initiatives that are likely to have the greatest benefit, the initiatives have already been selected to reflect stakeholders' opinions on "which [of them] will have the greatest potential for positive impact." EPA believes that no further prioritization in terms of impact is necessary; it does, however, rank its activities according to urgency. In so doing, it follows recommendation of NAS, which, in its second peer review of the Research Action Plan, said the Agency should "develop a prioritization framework to meet urgent needs for water-security research, while simultaneously preserving a longer-term research strategy. Key tasks that have relatively quick and immediate value should be given higher priority over longer-term projects that, while worthwhile, compete for human and financial resources." These specific activities and their time phasing will be shared with the DHS S&T Directorate and the White House's OSTP in a later version of this SSP.

The following R&D initiatives are taken from EPA's Research Action Plan and are grouped into seven overarching topics. As previously mentioned, while the plan was developed prior to establishment of the Water Sector's vision, goals, and objectives as identified in section 1 of this SSP, these goals and objectives do align with the R&D initiatives as well as the NCIP R&D Plan's themes and strategic goals. Most R&D priorities listed below, on some level, may support the sector's goals; each has been associated with its primary supporting goal(s). All these activities and linkages continue to help utilities be better prepared to prevent, detect, respond to, and recover from all hazards.

PRIORITY: Protecting Drinking Water Systems from Physical and Cyber Threats, supported by the Water Sector's goals 1 and 2. To address this priority, EPA is conducting security-related research in the following areas:

- Updating the identification and prioritization of physical threats and vulnerabilities of drinking water infrastructure;

- Understanding and documenting the consequences of physical or cyber attacks on the drinking water supply sources and infrastructure, including evaluation and testing of computational models and decision science; and

- Developing and/or improving a suite of countermeasures to prevent, or mitigate the effects of, physical and cyber attacks on water infrastructure, including improved design of SCADA and water systems to reduce vulnerabilities.

PRIORITY: Identifying Drinking Water Threats, Contaminants, and Threat Scenarios, supported by the Water Sector's goals 1 and 2. To address this priority, EPA is conducting security-related research in the following areas:

- Developing a manageable, prioritized list of threats, contaminants, and threat scenarios that might be used to destroy, disrupt, or disable drinking water supplies and systems;

- Developing a contaminant-identification tool for consultation by approved individuals and organizations that describes critically important information on contaminants that could harm drinking water supplies and systems;

- Identifying carefully selected surrogates or simulants for use in testing and evaluating fate-and-transport characteristics and treatment technologies for priority contaminants; and

- Developing methods and means to securely maintain and, when appropriate, transmit information on threats, contaminants, and threat scenarios applicable to drinking water supplies and systems.

PRIORITY: Improving Analytical Methodologies and Monitoring Systems for Drinking Water, supported by the Water Sector's goals 1, 2, and 3. To address this priority, EPA is conducting security-related research in the following areas to develop:

- A playbook (or module) for sampling and analytical response to contaminant threats and attacks on water supplies and systems, including protocols for identifying unknown contaminants, that will serve as a vital component of an integrated response plan;

- New analytical hardware and associated field and laboratory analysis methodologies for biological contaminants in water, including requirements for appropriate quality assurance/quality control (QA/QC) and sampling approaches;

- Improved analytical hardware and associated field and laboratory analysis methodologies for chemical contaminants in water, including requirements for appropriate QA/QC and sampling approaches;

- Monitoring technologies, including standard operating procedures, for biological, chemical, and radiological contaminants and threats;

- Drinking water early warning systems (EWSs), and EWSs from other sectors amenable to application in the water environment;

- Improved and expanded, tiered laboratory capacity and capability in order to be fully prepared to respond to threats or attacks on water;

- Training modules, drills, and evaluation exercises for analytical methodologies and monitoring systems; and

- Integrated and consolidated databases and analytical methodologies of other Federal agencies.

PRIORITY: Containing, Treating, Decontaminating, and Disposing of Contaminated Water and Materials, supported by the Water Sector's goals 2 and 3. To address this priority, EPA is conducting security-related research in the following areas to develop:

- Improved distribution system models that can be used to more effectively protect drinking water in case of deliberate contamination;

- Improved understanding and documentation of the environmental fate of contaminants in source waters, within drinking water plants, and in distribution systems;

- New and more effective treatment and decontamination technologies and processes for waters that have been contaminated; and

- Improved understanding and documentation of decontamination and disposal of pipes, equipment, and other materials, and of when a decontaminated system can be returned to safe use.

PRIORITY: Planning for Contingencies and Addressing Infrastructure Interdependencies, supported by the Water Sector's goal 3. To address this priority, EPA is conducting security-related research in the following areas to develop:

- Assessment and case studies of water supply alternatives for different types of drinking water systems in the United States (reflecting the effects of size, type of supply, system design, and type of distribution system) when the usual supply of water is not available;

- Improved technologies and approaches through tests and evaluations for providing supplies of water in case of long-term and short-term disruptions to drinking water systems; and

- Improved understanding of water system interdependencies and the relationships of such interdependencies with other infrastructure sectors critical to national security.

PRIORITY: Targeting Impacts on Human Health and Informing the Public about Risks is supported by the Water Sector's goals 3 and 4. To address this priority, EPA is conducting security-related research work in the following areas to develop:

- Improved understanding of multiple routes of exposure from contaminants in drinking water supplies and systems, which should focus on generic models for different large classes of contaminants, and an improved understanding of acute and short-term exposures and of chronic public health effects from contaminants in drinking water supplies and systems, which should focus on generic models for different large classes of contaminants;

- A health surveillance network to help public health officials and utility operators to rapidly identify and control disease outbreaks or other public health emergencies associated with contaminated drinking water;

- Evaluation of the usefulness and validity of nontraditional data sources (e.g., LD50 and quantitative structure activity relationship) for derivation of acute and chronic toxicity values applied to water);

- Risk assessment/risk management framework for identifying the impact of containment, decontamination, treatment, and disposal options, and the subsequent response; and

- Methods and means to communicate risks to local communities, and to respond to customers in case of an attack on drinking water systems.

PRIORITY: Wastewater Treatment and Collection System Protection, supported by the Water Sector's goal 2. To address this priority, EPA is conducting security-related research in the following areas to develop:

- A thorough understanding and documentation of possible threats to the Nation's wastewater treatment and collection systems, including the interdependencies of drinking water systems and other critical infrastructure;

- Updated assessment of the possible health, safety, and environmental risks related to potentially hazardous substances used by wastewater utilities or produced during responses to security threats (e.g., decontamination materials and their byproducts), or intentionally introduced into wastewater collection and treatment systems or storm water conveyance and treatment systems, including any impact on residuals management operations (sewage sludge);

- Improved intrusion monitoring and surveillance technologies to quickly notify wastewater utilities when these facilities or technologies are compromised by physical or cyber threats or by CBR contaminants;

- Improved designs for wastewater systems to reduce vulnerability to physical threats and prevent or mitigate the effects of attacks on wastewater infrastructure;

- Enhanced prevention and response planning methods, including emergency response (e.g., relocation of discharge or alternative treatment), contingency planning, and risk communication protocols and guidance for wastewater systems of varying types (size, geographic location, design); and

- Methods and means to securely maintain and, when appropriate, transmit information on contaminants and threat scenarios applicable to wastewater systems.

All activities are ongoing and future versions of this SSP will identify results as well as additional needs and gaps in the Water Sector's security R&D program.

Identification of Additional Security-Related Research Needs

The DHS has funded a project to develop needs related to water-security research. A report entitled the *"Domestic Municipal End-to-End Water Architecture Study,"* will be used by EPA, coordinating with the WSCC and GCC, to identify additional Water Sector research needs, note any areas where technologies meeting water-security requirements seem to be lacking, and request information on needs shared with other infrastructure sectors. After working with the coordinating councils, EPA will review the DHS's response and recommend priorities to be addressed by future inter-sector initiatives.

The Water Sector welcomes the opportunity to coordinate with the DHS in identifying needs between existing technology and current R&D initiatives. As described above, EPA has done considerable work to identify and fulfill the sector's technical requirements. The Agency also routinely surveys other sectors for applicable technologies. NHSRC, for example, follows developments in commercial, industrial, and military instrumentation for possible applications to water security. The Navy research program has developed mobile treatment units to supply drinking water, and EPA is working with the Navy to advance these technologies for use when water supplies are interrupted. The DHS's technological perspective across all infrastructure sectors will benefit the Agency in this effort.

As part of the collaborative SSP writing process, AwwaRF and WERF provided input on current R&D needs. Some of these needs were based on findings of the cosponsored EPA and WEF Water Security Workshops. Identified needs for additional R&D activities are described below:

Detection and Sensor Systems: Continuing research is needed to develop strategically placed, real-time, reliable, accurate, and affordable sensors that can provide early warning detection of harmful CBR contaminants introduced in the source water, collection/distribution networks, and treatment/discharge systems of water utilities. As a key part of this research, guidance should be developed for planning an Early Warning System Sensors implementation framework; the benefits to utilities should be clearly laid out to gain their acceptance. In this regard, operational protocols and associated training programs should be established for utility operators and managers. To address this issue in drinking water distribution systems, as directed by HSPD-9, EPA is piloting its Water Security Initiative to develop robust, comprehensive, and fully coordinated surveillance and monitoring systems to provide early detection and awareness of drinking water contamination, EPA has launched its Water Security Initiative in one select city. This demonstration project will design, deploy, and evaluate a model contamination warning system for drinking water security. The contaminant warning system involves active deployment and use of monitoring technologies/strategies, and enhanced surveillance activities to collect, integrate, analyze, and communicate information. For more information on this initiative, see section 5 of the SSP.

Continuing research is also needed to fill a significant knowledge gap regarding the potential harm, fate, and transport of priority CBR contaminants of concern in wastewater liquid and sludge/biosolids that could have a significant impact on land application practices and the Food and Agriculture Sector. Effective means to prevent deliberate backflow of contaminants into water distribution systems should also be studied.

Protection and Prevention: Cyber security is an important cross-sector issue dealing with protection of enterprise information systems from outside or inside attack. Though the Water Sector can operate independent of SCADA control systems, its heavy use of automated operations could result in negative public health and economic impacts following a successful cyber attack. With support of the DHS's NCSD, two sector security partners, WERF and AwwaRF, in close collaboration with EPA, are developing a self-assessment tool for SCADA control systems for water utilities to embrace uniform cross-sector architecture security-related specifications for process control systems. There will be a need for tool validation, maintenance, and training for successful and widespread implementation by utilities. The DHS, EPA, WERF, and AwwaRF will continue to work closely to address cyber security needs in the sector.

Advanced Infrastructure Architectures and System Designs: The Water Sector infrastructure components (collection network, distribution network, etc.) are widely dispersed over a large physical area, a significant challenge for undertaking intrusion detection and surveillance operations. Innovations are needed in development of the next generation of facility monitoring, control, and communication networks, including design of "smart pipes" and "intelligent infrastructure." Real-time operational control, aided by cross-sensor and cross-system information collection, is a significant part of this research. The research will also focus on continuity of service and resiliency for uninterrupted provision of safe water and wastewater services to the public and maintenance for firefighting capabilities.

Decision Support Tools: Consideration should be given to formulating a value-chain model of a wastewater utility as the basis for understanding where and how security improvement and risk management practices affect decision-making. Using this model, one can document how wastewater utilities currently use security and risk management practices and whether they benefit the utility, its customers, and/or the community.

People/Culture Issues: EPA's three water security workshops identified the importance of creating and maintaining a "security culture" at the utility as part of normal business practices. Although the Water Sector has worked diligently for 30-plus years to ensure that those entrusted with the day-to-day operations of a utility are consistently educated on the value and purpose of security at their facilities, developing and distributing effective education tools and outreach materials remains a critical priority.

EPA will work closely with the WSCC, GCC, and the DHS to develop R&D initiatives that meet technology needs in the sector. Some of the same challenges outlined previously in this SSP also impact Water Sector R&D efforts; for more information on these challenges see section 6. A number of needs, particularly those related to physical and cyber security can be addressed across sectors. Needs related to contaminant threats to water supplies and systems are more limited in their cross-sector application. Contamination of water with CBR agents presents unique challenges when compared to the vast majority of other sectors. The sector most related to the Water Sector is Food and Agriculture, led by USDA (USDA shares SSA responsibility with the FDA for the sector). EPA will continue to work closely with the CDC to address contaminant threats associated with water.

EPA's process for soliciting candidate R&D initiatives from the DHS S&T Directorate and the White House's OSTP will parallel its process for soliciting technology requirements. EPA, after coordinating with the WSCC and GCC, will submit to the S&T Directorate and OSTP a preliminary set of candidate R&D initiatives. This set will result from the process used to generate the Research Action Plan, supplemented by the needs analysis jointly developed by EPA, the S&T Directorate, and OSTP. EPA will note any areas in which it is unaware of R&D initiatives suitable for filling the stated needs, and in which it requests information on such initiatives taking place in other infrastructure sectors. Using the established NIPP partnership model, the WSCC and GCC will review the DHS's responses and recommend priorities to be addressed by future inter-sector initiatives.

7.4 R&D Management Processes

The Water Sector will pursue a focused, coordinated approach to developing research initiatives that align with its stated goals and objectives, to accomplish clearly defined activities, projects, and initiatives that contain time-based deliverables tied to priority R&D requirements. The WSCC is an established body that represents the sector, has good sector representation, strong cross-sector coordination, and serves as the starting point for defining organizational roles and leadership. Its counterpart, the GCC, provides an established body for coordinating government efforts among the DHS, EPA, and other relevant Federal and State agencies. Both councils are integral parts of the R&D vetting and review process.

EPA has the lead in managing the R&D aspects of the Water SSP, but as noted previously, it fully engages and collaborates with sector security partners for input and development of priorities. EPA will collaborate within the GCC and WSCC partnership framework to update the Water Sector R&D plan. The extensive process that EPA used to create its Research Action Plan has established a baseline that will facilitate annual updates of the Agency's portion of the NCIP R&D Plan. EPA will circulate the Research Action Plan to a similar panel of stakeholders in a form that allows them to note any changed priorities, additions, or deletions. When appropriate and necessary, the revised plan will be forwarded to the DHS S&T Directorate and OSTP for incorporation into the NCIP R&D Plan. The Research Action Plan will be aligned with the sector's goals and objectives as well as the nine technology themes and three strategic goals articulated in the NCIP R&D Plan.

EPA, other government agencies, and private organizations are pursuing many of the initiatives jointly; using a collaborative approach to research increases the likelihood that initiatives with the greatest potential for positive impacts are being pursued.

Collaboration With the DHS

EPA is collaborating in several ways with the DHS S&T Directorate to develop and execute security-related research. NHSRC has met with DHS representatives to address security R&D in the Water Sector. Interactions began with the S&T Directorate in December 2002; these interactions have resulted in a series of cross-briefings on water-security research. The DHS's Infrastructure Subcommittee (ISC), in conjunction with all SSAs, was established to develop consensus and resolve issues related to R&D for infrastructure protection. EPA is participating on the ISC support team that developed the NCIP R&D Plan, and is taking measures to ensure that these parallel efforts under HSPD-7 are coordinated within the Agency. There are also two interagency working groups (IWGs) that are supporting the ISC in this planning effort: the Physical Structures and Systems IWG and Critical Information Infrastructure Protection IWG. EPA, in collaboration with its Water Sector security partners, is also working with the DHS to better understand and share threat information that may result in development of additional research projects. The annual NCIP R&D Plan will address R&D programs and requirements across Federal agencies, from the critical infrastructure sector owner/operators, and from international organizations such as the Global Water Research Coalition. The NCIP R&D Plan will also integrate R&D plans across the physical and cyber domains.

Collaboration With CDC

NHSRC and CDC are jointly pursuing research on treatment efficacy for a range of biological contaminants and biotoxins. Work between CDC and NHSRC researchers is expected to continue for the foreseeable future; CDC and EPA work closely to deliver information on contaminant threats to the WaterISAC.

Work in a new area is now being carried out by several of CDC's institutes and EPA. A workshop for drinking water utilities and public health officials explored the feasibility of public health surveillance as a means to warn of contaminant attacks on drinking water systems. The workshop was held, and a number of water utilities and public health organizations participated. In many instances, the invitees represented both the water utility and public health officials in the same city (e.g., New York City and Seattle). CDC and EPA are now undertaking a pilot program in a select location to test the feasibility of this approach.

EPA is working with CDC and other agencies to develop devices to facilitate collection and concentration of samples from large volumes of water. These devices are components in laboratory collection of drinking water samples for pathogen detection. In addition, this work involves development of presumptive laboratory methods for analysis of pathogens in water.

EPA is working with CDC to form an alliance of drinking water laboratories for integration with CDC's LRN. The result is the WLA, which supports implementation of HSPD-9's requirements. Where appropriate, EPA is also collaborating with USDA and FDA to identify options for leveraging components of FERN to further support requirements of HSPD-9.

Collaboration With Others

Other Federal agencies that EPA works with on R&D are DOD, USACE, FDA, DOE national laboratories, USGS, and other applicable parts within EPA such as the Threat Ensemble Vulnerability Assessment (TEVA) Program and the Technology Testing and Evaluation Program (TTEP). EPA also works with AwwaRF, WERF, and the National Sanitation Foundation. Many of these organizations have been brought together, under EPA sponsorship, in the DSRC. Funding has been provided through EPA to AwwaRF and WERF to develop tools and conduct research on drinking water and wastewater security issues, respectively. EPA is collaborating with the American Society of Civil Engineers, AWWA, and WEF to finalize voluntary physical security standards; utility owner/operators will be better prepared to prevent, detect, respond to, and recover from manmade and naturally occurring events.

NHSRC cooperated with AWWA to create a Water Contaminant Detection Working Group. EPA is supporting this effort by participating in organizational meetings and providing program advice and insights on HSPDs 7, 9, and 10. The water utilities in the working group will work with NHSRC staff to test technologies and research results in the field. An organizational meeting was held in 2004, a second meeting in January 2005, and a third in September 2006.

EPA will work with the Water Sector to monitor R&D progress, assess its impact on the sector goals, and update its R&D strategy as needed. To accomplish this, EPA will continue to work with the GCC, WSCC, as well as the international community. It will also keep apprised of non-sector-specific R&D efforts that could benefit the Water Sector through information provided by the DHS S&T Directorate, OSTP and others. EPA will continue to identify new technology requirements through the processes discussed above. Furthermore, through other vehicles such as third-party review of documents, EPA will survey reports of other offices and agencies to identify technology need areas. It has already reviewed many, including a lessons-learned report from implementation of vulnerability analyses and GAO recommendations on how funding should be allocated for drinking water and wastewater infrastructure protection.

Also, EPA staff conducts ongoing internal analysis of threats and technologies to identify shortcomings, weaknesses, and additional needs. EPA will continue to develop its understanding of Water Sector vulnerabilities through analysis of physical and cyber systems and contaminant and threat scenarios. This effort improves and focuses the Agency's ability to address the sector's most pressing research needs. Finally, EPA staff continually surveys external research activities and reviews developments in water security technology by reading published papers, meeting individually with researchers, and attending and supporting conferences on water security. This process actively engages individuals and organizations that conduct R&D related to high-priority needs in protecting water infrastructure.

The transition process from R&D to implementing the technology for protection programs in the field is also critical to the success of R&D efforts. Each technology will require at least a slightly different implementation path. However, in most cases there will be a pilot project where the technology is implemented in the field prior to widespread use. EPA will work with sector security partners to identify the best implementation process for a given technology.

8. Managing and Coordinating Sector-Specific Agency Responsibilities

This section of the SSP addresses how EPA will manage its SSA responsibilities, the processes for maintaining and updating the Water SSP, how sector annual reporting requirements related to CI/KR protection will be satisfied, resource allocation, sector CI/KR protection training and education, implementation of the sector partnership model, and how information will be shared and protected.

8.1 Program Management Approach

Prior to September 11, EPA began a more focused collaborative process with Water Sector security partners to address requirements of PDD-63. In response to September 11 and with passage of the Bioterrorism Act, EPA expanded its security planning and established OHS within its Office of the Administrator, the WSD within its Office of Water (OW), and the NHSRC within its Office of Research and Development. Furthermore, the Office of Solid Waste and Emergency Response (OSWER), which has always dealt with emergency response, expanded its mission to deal with homeland security-related activities.

OHS's mission is to lead and coordinate homeland security activities and policy development across all EPA program areas, while ensuring consistent direction and facilitating effective communication of homeland security efforts both within and outside the Agency. OHS is charged by the Administrator with major areas of responsibility:

- Serving as the Agency-wide point of contact to the White House Homeland Security Council and the DHS;

- Updating, facilitating, and tracking implementation of the EPA Homeland Security Strategy;

- Establishing a more centralized and efficient system for receiving and evaluating important homeland security classified communications from multiple sources;

- Establishing IT systems that provide the latest information on Agency efforts on homeland security projects; and

- Supporting program offices' and regional offices' ability to do "business as usual" while absorbing their new homeland security responsibilities.

WSD takes the lead for and aligns all national and Water Sector strategic planning and program management efforts. EPA's Water Sector security mission is to provide national leadership in developing and promoting security programs that enhance the sector's all-hazards approach: to prevent, detect, respond to, and recover from potential terrorist attacks, other intentional acts, natural disasters, and other hazards.

NHSRC manages, coordinates, and supports various security-related research and technical assistance efforts. It develops and delivers reliable, responsive expertise and products based on scientific research and technology evaluation. The work conducted and the products created by NHSRC are widely used to prevent, detect, respond to, and recover from public health and environmental emergencies arising from terrorist threats, other intentional threats, and natural disasters.

EPA's OSWER is actively involved in counterterrorism planning and response efforts and continues to prepare for and will respond to terrorist threats from weapons of mass destruction that have the capability to cause death or serious bodily injury to a significant number of people through release, dissemination, or impact of toxic poisonous chemicals; disease organisms; or radiation or radioactivity. Because of its inherent role in protecting human health and the environment from possible harmful effects of certain CBR materials, OSWER supports national homeland security-related efforts by: (1) helping State and local responders plan for emergencies, (2) coordinating with key Federal partners, (3) training first-responders, and (4) providing resources in a manmade or naturally occurring incident.

All these EPA offices have worked together and created a robust CIP program; work continues to maintain and improve on these protection activities. WSD manages all SSA responsibilities for the Water Sector. NHSRC and WSD provide each other with the support and technical assistance needed to advance research-related security projects and programs that primarily affect the Water Sector (NHSRC research projects do have impacts on other sectors). OHS provides guidance and support to WSD, NHSRC, and OSWER at the policy level. The relationship between these EPA offices is depicted below in figure 8-1.

Figure 8-1: EPA Security-Related Organizational Chart

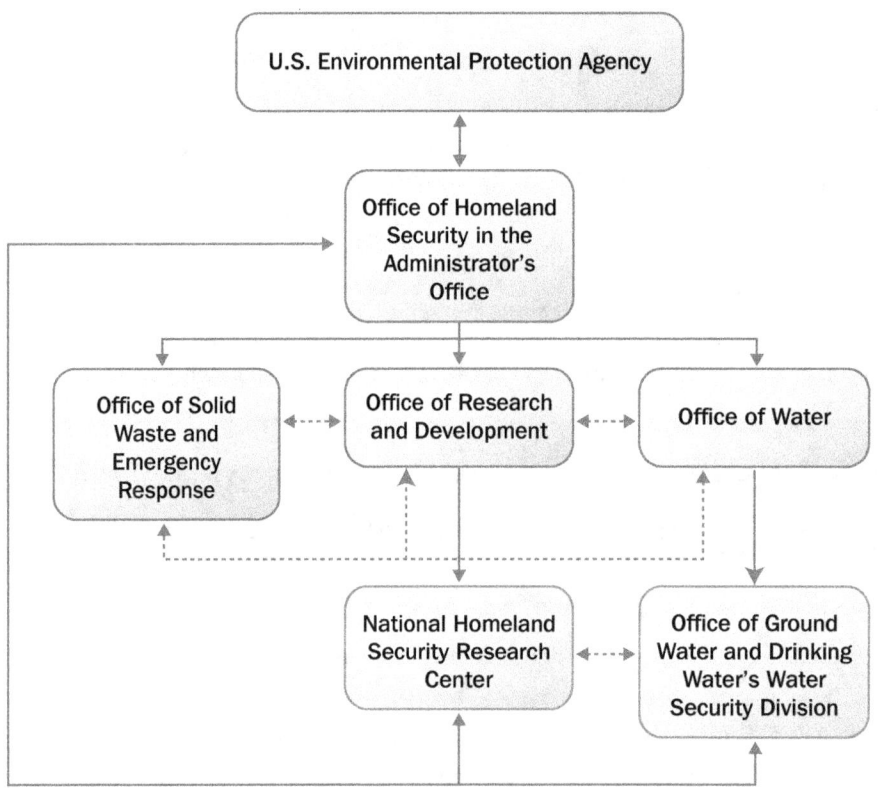

EPA's responsibility as the SSA for the Water Sector involves: (1) collaborating with all relevant Federal departments and agencies, State and local governments, and the private sector; (2) conducting or facilitating vulnerability assessments of the sector; and (3) encouraging risk management strategies to protect against and mitigate the effects of all-hazards attacks against CI/KR.

This includes collaborating with sector security partners and supporting sector-coordinating mechanisms to: (1) identify, prioritize, and coordinate protection of CI/KR; and (2) facilitate sharing of information and physical and cyber threats, vulnerabilities, incidents, potential protective measures, and best practices.

To implement its requirements under HSPD-7, the DHS collaborated with all SSAs and Water Sector security partners to develop the NIPP. The establishment of the NIPP resulted in the following responsibilities for EPA: (1) supporting NIPP concepts, (2) coordinating funding and implementation programs that enhance CI/KR protection, (3) coordinating development of the SSP in collaboration with sector security partners, (4) undertaking measures outlined in the NIPP Implementation Initiatives and Actions matrix, (5) developing and maintaining partnerships with security partners, and (6) protecting critical information according to authorities and guidelines. To ensure coordination and collaboration around these NIPP-related requirements, EPA is working with its Federal, State, tribal, and local government partners, national and State associations, and its WSCC and GCC.

EPA is encouraging and helping to fund development of appropriate information-sharing and analysis mechanisms within the sector that can further communication. This includes supporting the WaterISAC and WaterSC. The WaterISAC is currently evaluating the DHS's cross-sector communication mechanism, HSIN, examining how integrating it within the WaterISAC might serve utilities by facilitating the sharing of information on physical and cyber threats, vulnerabilities, incidents, recommended protective measures, and security-related best practices. Further coordination includes encouraging voluntary sharing of security-related information, where possible, among public and private entities and security partners, helping to better assure timely and data-driven decision-making.

In addition, EPA maintains regular and frequent communication with its Water Sector security partners. For example, monthly conference calls are held with all security partnering organizations, and quarterly face-to-face meetings are held with this same group. In the past, EPA has held numerous sector coordination workshops, and WSD staff regularly attend workshops and conferences to provide information on sector security activities and policies. Furthermore, EPA has 10 regional offices throughout the Nation; a security point of contact exists in every regional office, and regular coordination conference calls and activities occur between these points of contact and the EPA Headquarters office. Finally, the Agency also participates in all GCC meetings and with the WSCC as appropriate. More details about sector security partner relationships can be found in section 1 of this SSP.

EPA will use the NIPP partnership model to implement the Water Sector's security goals and objectives. EPA will continue to use this partnership model to develop and refine protective programs to better prepare utilities to prevent, detect, respond to, and recover from terrorist attacks, other intentional acts, natural disasters, and other hazards.

8.2 Processing and Responsibilities

8.2.1 SSP Maintenance and Update

EPA, in concert with the GCC and WSCC, is responsible for ensuring that the Water SSP is completed and updated based on significant events, changes in the sector's security posture, or changes in the approach to securing the sector. The Water SSP is a planning document that is collaboratively developed using the NIPP partnership model. The NIPP is a multiyear plan describing mechanisms for sustaining the Nation's steady-state protective posture. It and the component SSPs include a process for annual review; periodic interim updates as required; and will be reissued every three years, or more frequently, if directed by the Secretary of Homeland Security. EPA is committed to working with the WSCC and GCC to coordinate the annual review and triennial update of the Water SSP. The SSP revision process will include developing or updating any documents necessary to carry out NIPP activities.

8.2.2 Annual Reporting

Annually, on July 1, SSAs are required to submit a report to the DHS detailing their sector's efforts to identify, prioritize, and coordinate protection of CI/KR. These Sector CI/KR Protection Annual Reports are used by the DHS to inform the National CI/KR Protection Annual Report. For July 2006, EPA submitted a Sector Annual Report based on DHS guidance that included information in the following subject areas: (1) Sector Security Goals, Priorities, and Requirements; (2) Sector Programs and Initiatives; (3) Funding Priorities; and (4) Program Effectiveness and Continuous Improvement. In the future, EPA will work closely with the GCC and WSCC to develop and submit these annual reports to the DHS. Each year's report will at least include updates on the above-mentioned subject areas. EPA intends to begin the annual report process in the early part of each year to ensure there is adequate time to engage with the WSCC and GCC.

8.2.3 Resources and Budgets

Given the variety of Federal, State, local, tribal, and public/private sector security partners that contribute funds and other resources to protect the Water Sector, neither EPA nor any other entity has authority over resources and budgets for the entire sector. While EPA can describe the Federal Water Sector contribution, it does not have a complete or accurate picture of the resources its sector security partners are allocating. These non-SSA investments are projected to be substantial. EPA continues to work with its security partners to provide information on available SSA resources and budget information. All these groups will coordinate to develop and share recommendations regarding allocation of sector resources and related funding. EPA's programmatic planning will be guided by the goals outlined in this SSP. These recommendations will be based on the strategic approach outlined in section 5 and on analysis of the cost effectiveness and reduction of risk associated with security-related expenditures.

Throughout each summer's planning process, OW, in conjunction with other EPA offices and divisions, will develop the recommended EPA budget requests for Water Sector security and related training expenditures. The Agency's annual budget request is submitted to the Office of Management and Budget (OMB) on the second Tuesday of each September. Between September and November, OW will work with the DHS and OMB to provide supporting documentation specific to EPA's request. Based on the initial submission and support documentation, OMB, coordinating with the DHS, provides final decisions late in the calendar year regarding EPA's budget and resources available for sector security and related training. EPA will work closely with security partners to promote the most efficient use of these Federal expenditures, and will offer its expertise to help the public and private sectors maximize the effectiveness of the resources allocated to sector security and preparedness. EPA will initiate the coordination efforts with sector security partners during the February through June timeframe of each fiscal year to prepare the budget section of the Annual Report. EPA consults closely with its security partners in implementing the water security program initiatives.

8.2.4 Training and Education

Successful implementation of the national risk management framework relies on building and maintaining individual and organizational CI/KR protection expertise. Training and education in a variety of areas is necessary to achieve and sustain this level of expertise. EPA has already initiated a robust training program developed to provide specific instruction tailored to the size and type of a given Water Sector utility. This training will be tailored in the future to complement the vision, goals, and objectives identified by the sector and will focus on the Nation's largest utilities. Training provided may focus on areas such as risk evaluation and assessments, response and recovery exercises, establishment of mutual networks, and other security-related topics. Sector security partners will greatly benefit from continued training and education.

EPA, in collaboration with its security partners, will continue to provide the Water Sector with the tools, classroom training, and technical assistance it needs to be better prepared to prevent, detect, respond to, and recover from terrorist attacks, other intentional acts, natural disasters, and other hazards. Such functions may include providing exercises to improve emergency response planning, information on how to detect and treat high-priority contaminants, and voluntary guidelines for enhancing physical and cyber security. Many utilities have well-developed ERPs and test emergency response capabilities on a regular basis to continuously improved their protective posture. Section 6.2 of the NIPP lists some of the areas of expertise where training is recommended, examples of currently available training, and other general information on CI/KR protection-related training and education. EPA will work with the DHS and other security partners to identify additional training needs and support them based on availability of funds. For more information on training programs supported by EPA and its sector security partners, see appendix 3 of this SSP.

8.3 Implementing the Sector Partnership Model

SSAs are responsible for collaborating with public and private sector security partners and encouraging development of appropriate information-sharing and analysis mechanisms within the sector. This includes coordination with State and local governments, as well as other Federal partners such as the DHS, FBI, and CIA. Under DHS direction and guidance, EPA coordinates security efforts per the NIPP sector partnership model, which includes the WSCC and GCC, to seek input and direction and to identify gaps and next steps for CIP activities.

The Private Sector Cross-Sector Council (i.e., the Partnership for Critical Infrastructure Security); the Government Cross-Sector Council (made up of two sub councils: the NIPP Federal Senior Leadership Council (FSLC) and the State, Local, and Tribal Government Coordinating Council (SLTGCC)); and individual SCCs and GCCs create a structure through which representative groups from Federal, State, local, and tribal governments, sector partners, and public and private critical infrastructure owner/operators can collaborate and develop consensus approaches to CI/KR protection. EPA is using this NIPP partnership model as a collaborative mechanism for the government and Water Sector security partners to work together to better prepare the sector to prevent, detect, respond to, and recover from manmade or naturally occurring events. Through the GCC and WSCC, sector security partners will facilitate cross-cutting planning, policy-setting, coordination, and information sharing to identify cost-effective, efficient, and targeted approaches for developing and implementing security programs based on a risk management framework.

Figure 8-2 illustrates how the 17 CI/KR sectors are implementing the partnership model and how coordination is taking place across sectors. If applicable, regional councils will be developed.

Figure 8-2: DHS Sector Partnership Model

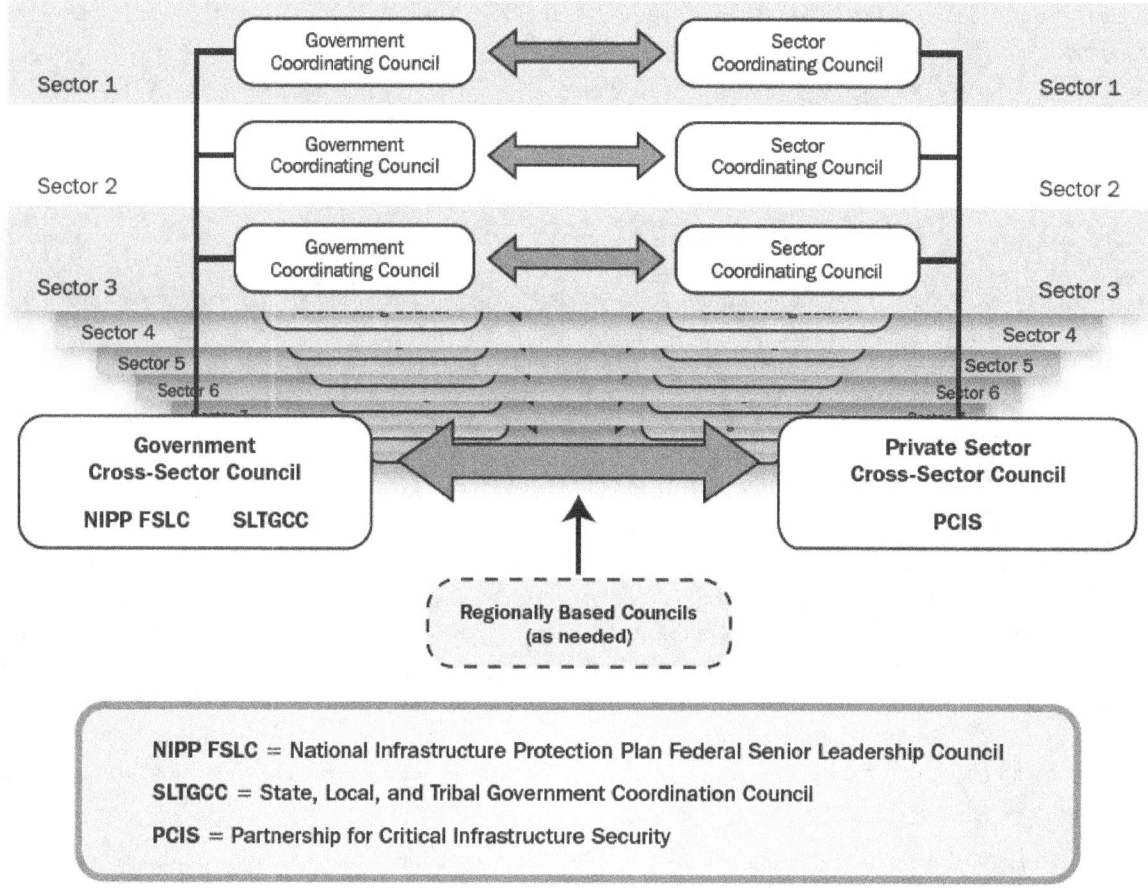

NIPP FSLC = National Infrastructure Protection Plan Federal Senior Leadership Council

SLTGCC = State, Local, and Tribal Government Coordination Council

PCIS = Partnership for Critical Infrastructure Security

8.3.1 NIPP Coordinating Structures

EPA and the DHS facilitated formation of the GCC in 2005. The GCC is comprised of representatives across various levels of government as appropriate to the security landscape of the Water Sector. The GCC is chaired by EPA, which has responsibility for ensuring appropriate representation on the GCC and providing cross-sector coordination with State and local governments. Each GCC is co-chaired by the DHS Assistant Secretary for Infrastructure Protection or his/her designee. The GCC coordinates strategies, activities, policy, and communications across government entities within each sector. The primary functions of the GCC include providing interagency strategic communications and coordination at the sector level through partnership with the DHS; EPA; other supporting Federal departments and agencies; and State, tribal, and local governments. The GCC also partici-pates in planning related to development, implementation, update, and revision of the NIPP and SSPs; coordinating strategic communications and issue management and resolution among government entities within the sector; and coordinating with and supporting the efforts of the WSCC to plan, implement, and execute the Nation's CI/KR protection mission.

The GCC provides effective coordination of CI/KR strategies and activities, policy, and communication across government and between the government and the Water Sector to support the Nation's homeland security mission. In addition, the GCC coordinates with and supports the efforts of the WSCC and EPA to plan, implement, and execute sufficient and necessary sec-tor-wide security. It serves to leverage complementary resources within government and between government and industry.

Official members named to the GCC are director-level or equivalent representatives from the following: the DHS (FEMA), DoD (USACE), DOI (BuRec), FERC, DOS, EPA, HHS (CDC and OPHEP), USDA, ASDWA, and ASIWPCA.

In 2004, eight drinking water and wastewater associations (AMWA, AWWA, AwwaRF, NACWA, NAWC, NRWA, WEF, and WERF) formed the WSCC. The WSCC is comprised of water utility managers appointed by these associations and members of the associations. It serves as a policy, strategy, and coordination mechanism, and recommends actions to reduce and eliminate significant security vulnerabilities of the Water Sector through interaction with the Federal government and other critical infrastructure sectors. As members of the WSCC, the associations serve as a liaison among the WSCC, GCC, and broader Water Sector community.

The WSCC enables owner/operators to interact on a wide range of sector-specific strategies, policies, activities, and issues, and serves as the principal sector policy coordination and planning entity. It also relies on the WaterISAC and other information-sharing mechanisms that provide operational and tactical capabilities for information sharing and, in some cases, support for incident response activities. The purpose of the WSCC includes representing a point-of-entry for government into the sector to address the entire range of CI/KR protection activities and issues for that sector. The WSCC serves as a strategic communications and coordination mechanism between CI/KR owners, operators, and suppliers, and with the government during response and recovery as determined by the sector and identifies, implements, and supports the information-sharing capabilities and mechanisms that are most appropriate for the sector. The WaterISAC may perform this role if so designated by the WSCC.

The WSCC serves as the mechanism to facilitate organization and coordination of the sector's CI/KR policy development, infrastructure protection planning, and coordination of implementation activities with EPA and the DHS. Such activities include planning, development of sector best practices, adoption of protective programs and plans, development of requirements for effective information sharing, R&D, and cross-sector coordination. EPA and the DHS will coordinate all program development activities in the sector through the coordinating councils.

In addition, joint meetings of the WSCC and GCC are covered under CIPAC, which directly supports the sector partnership model by providing a legal framework for members of the SCCs and GCCs to engage in joint CI/KR protection-related activities. The Chairman of either the WSCC or GCC can facilitate and organize joint council meetings in consultation with the chairman of the other council. The CIPAC serves as a forum for government and public and private sector security partners to engage in a broad spectrum of activities, such as planning, coordination, implementation, and operational issues; implementation of security programs; operational activities related to CI/KR protection, including incident response, recovery, and reconstitution; and development and support of national plans, including the NIPP and the SSPs.

8.3.2 State and Local Government Entities (Regional) Coordination

EPA depends heavily on State drinking water primacy agencies and the wastewater permitting authorities that implement the SDWA and CWA. As mentioned in previous chapters, the water sector is comprised of both drinking water and wastewater assets and has a long history of implementing programs to protect public health and the environment under the SDWA and CWA. Because almost all drinking water and wastewater programs are delegated to the States, EPA works with the States to ensure implementation of programmatic and security-related initiatives. In addition to Federal programmatic responsibilities, States have their own initiatives and priorities. State programs maintain inventories of drinking water and wastewater facilities, regularly inspect these systems, provide technical assistance, maintain laboratory and operator certification programs, and monitor compliance by reviewing analytical results. States review and approve plans and specifications for new and expanded facilities, and they take enforcement actions as needed. EPA is coordinating its security efforts and initiatives with State and local entities that represent the Water Sector. This coordination includes facilitating meetings, seeking input on sector security concerns and issues, and raising security awareness. Many of these entities are used as conduits to get information and training opportunities to utilities. For example, EPA provides security grants to State primacy agencies to enhance communication and coordination with utilities. Two of the main State-related organizations that EPA works with are ASDWA and ASIWPCA, which represent drinking water and wastewater programs in the States, District of Columbia, Territories, and commonwealths across the United States.

Regional partnerships, groupings, and governance bodies such as the SLTGCC will enable CI/KR protection coordination among security partners within and across geographical areas and sectors. The DHS is setting up these councils now. Such bodies will be composed of representatives from industry and State and local entities located in whole or part within the planning area for an aggregation of high-risk targets, urban areas, or cross-sector groupings. They will be organized to take common approaches to a wide variety of natural or manmade hazards. They will facilitate coordination between jurisdictions within a State where CI/KR cross multiple jurisdictions, and help sectors to coordinate with multiple States that rely on a common set of CI/KR. Regional organizations, whether interstate or intrastate, vary widely in terms of mission, composition, and functionality. Regardless of the variations, these organizations will provide structures at the strategic and/or operational levels that help address cross-sector CI/KR planning and protection program implementation. In many instances, State homeland security advisors serve as focal points for regional initiatives and provide linkages between the regional organizations and partnerships established under the NIPP framework. Based on the nature or focus of the regional initiative, these organizations may link into the sector partnership model, as appropriate, through individual SCCs or GCCs or cross-sector councils.

8.3.3 International

Some Water Sector CI/KR assets within the United States are interconnected with Mexico or Canada's infrastructure, supporting the economies on both sides of the border. The NIPP strategy for international CI/KR protection and coordination is focused on instituting effective cooperation with international security partners, as well as high-priority cross-border protective programs. Specific protective actions are developed through the sector planning process and specified in SSPs; they address cross-sector and global issues such as cyber security and foreign investment.

The Security and Prosperity Partnership of North America was launched in March 2005 as a trilateral effort to increase security and enhance prosperity through greater cooperation and information sharing among the United States, Canada, and Mexico. The initiative is premised on the nations' security and our economic prosperity being mutually reinforcing. The partnership recognizes that these three great nations are bound by a shared belief in freedom, economic opportunity, and strong democratic institutions, and provides the framework to ensure that North America is the safest and best place to live and do business. It includes ambitious security and prosperity programs to keep our borders closed to terrorism yet open to trade. The Security and Prosperity Partnership builds upon, but is separate from, these countries' longstanding trade and economic relationships and energizes other aspects of this cooperative relationship, such as protection of our environment, food supply, and public health. Looking forward, the countries have identified emergency management; influenza pandemics, including avian influenza; energy security; and safe and secure gateways (border security and facilitation) as priorities for the Security and Prosperity Partnership. Currently, and when and where appropriate, EPA is participating in activities related to the partnership. In addition, section 1 of this SSP contains other information on international Water Sector security concerns.

8.4 Information Sharing and Information Collection and Protection

A necessary component of the sector partnership model is information sharing and protection. The dissemination of important and relevant security information, such as physical and cyber threats, vulnerabilities, incidents, protective measures, and best practices, among Federal, State, and local governments occurs on an as-needed basis. While the GCC and WSCC framework is an effective way for government and sector security partners to communicate and coordinate efforts, there are additional mechanisms that foster good communication and information sharing. Sections 4, 5, and 6 of this SSP identify information-sharing mechanisms currently in place among security partners to share and protect information. EPA is responsible for collaboration with its security partners, as well as for encouraging development of information sharing and analysis processes and mechanisms to support these processes.

8.4.1 Information Sharing

There are multiple ways that the DHS, EPA, and Water Sector share unclassified and classified information. Through Web sites, partner updates, e-mail trees, Web casts, and other mechanisms, the sector is able to share unclassified security-related information (more information on these mechanisms can be found in appendix 4). The WaterISAC and WaterSC have been established in the Water Sector to receive secure classified information relevant to protection of the sector. As stated earlier, the DHS has started to pilot HSIN, a network that will provide secure communications across all critical infrastructure sectors. As HSIN begins operation, the WaterISAC will examine use of HSIN to better serve utilities. All these information-sharing mechanisms (WaterISAC, WaterSC, and HSIN) are discussed below.

The WaterISAC became operational in December 2002 and is funded by EPA and subscriber fees. It was developed to provide America's drinking water and wastewater utilities with a highly secure, Web-based environment for warning of potential physical, contamination, and cyber threats, and for information about security. The WaterISAC provides a unique link between the Water Sector and Federal environmental, homeland security, law enforcement, intelligence, and public health agencies. It offers communication and information tools such as public bulletins and advisories for both national and specific security alerts for the sector. WaterISAC subscribers are quickly notified of the latest government alerts on water security and receive expert analysis about how a reported threat may impact their water system.

The WaterISAC functions are routinely coordinated with the DHS and EPA as they pertain to data sharing, correlation, and safeguarding in cooperative analysis to identify and effectively respond to threats to utilities. Goals for continued daily WaterISAC coordination include: Continuing to improve methods of receiving information from utilities through the WaterSC, as well as coordinating and sharing information and intelligence with the industry; seeking utility-related industry participation in the WaterISAC; holding intelligence analyst meetings to review threat levels on at least a quarterly basis; providing the WaterISAC access to the National Incident Command Center and to information and intelligence relating to sector security; and using WaterISAC communication networks as a primary or alternative method of communication with private sector owner/operators and State primacy agencies.

More than 1,000 people, including CEOs and general managers with security responsibilities, at hundreds of large and small drinking water and wastewater systems currently subscribe to the WaterISAC. Most State drinking water primacy agencies are ISAC subscribers, this membership provides a mechanism to reach small and medium drinking water systems. Efforts are currently underway to expand that number. The WaterISAC is also exploring the possibility of providing international service.

A supplementary service, the WaterSC, has been added to the WaterISAC to reach a larger Water Sector audience. The WaterSC is an e-mail notification service and Web site that is a free and password-protected information-sharing portal for utilities. The WaterSC sends e-mail alerts on security issues from EPA and the DHS directly to a much larger group of utilities; it currently has more than 11,000 subscribers.

HSIN is a secure, Web-based, national communications platform that enables security partners to communicate and share near real-time information with each other and the DHS. HSIN is composed of multiple, nonhierarchical Communities of Interest). This structure allows government and industry partners to engage in collaborative exchanges based on specific information and security requirements, mission emphasis, or interest level. HSIN-Critical Infrastructure supports exchange of threat information to critical infrastructure owner/operators, first-responders, and local officials. HSIN also contains a Critical Infrastructure Warning Information Network, which is a private government network within HSIN that provides mission-critical connectivity and a survivable DHS capability for information sharing, collaboration, and alerts to Federal, State, and local agencies for critical infrastructure restoration when primary forms of communication are unavailable.

The DHS, coordinating with the FBI, CIA, and other intelligence agencies, is responsible for sharing critical infrastructure threat-related information with sector partners; EPA, as the Water Sector lead, where and when appropriate will assist the DHS in sharing this type of information. To help the sector better understand its threats, the DHS, FBI, and EPA have provided a classified threat briefing to those with clearances on the WSCC and GCC. In addition, recently the DHS, CIA, FBI, and EPA created an Unclassified/For Official Use Only document that identifies a threat in the sector and that is shared only with those in the sector that need to know. Through the Joint Terrorism Task Force program, the FBI shares information with local law enforcement and other sector security partners regarding specific threat information and investigations involving terrorism (for which FBI is the lead agency).

8.4.2 Information Collection and Protection

Protective programs in the Water Sector are not mandatory. Collection, verification, validation, storage, protection, and tracking of sector security information and measurements of progress are voluntary. The role of utilities relative to information collection includes providing subject matter expertise and operational, vulnerability, and consequence data. Furthermore, utilities have the option to report, through the WaterISAC and WaterSC, suspicious actions that could signal pre-operational terrorist activity.

Information voluntarily submitted by utilities and shared with the Federal government (e.g., the DHS and EPA), including information protected by the PCII Program or other approaches, will be integrated with government-collected information by the DHS and other intelligence agencies to produce comprehensive threat assessments and warning products. Important to note is that non-sensitive data collected in EPA's public databases (e.g., SDWIS and PCS) are publicly available, and community drinking water system vulnerability assessments, as mandated by the Bioterrorism Act, are protected from use and/or release. As required by the Bioterrorism Act, EPA developed a protocol to secure risk assessments submitted by community drinking water systems. Anyone who knowingly reveals an assessment or information derived from one is subject to criminal penalties.

As mentioned above, the PCII Program provides a mechanism for utilities to voluntarily submit security-related data to the Federal Government. The program was established pursuant to the Critical Infrastructure Information (CII) Act of 2002. The act creates a framework that enables private sector members to voluntarily submit sensitive information regarding the Nation's infrastructure to the DHS with assurance that it will be protected from public disclosure. The Act allows the DHS to share this information with other government entities that have homeland security responsibilities. The DHS established the PCII Program Office to manage information, develop protocols for how to care for "voluntarily submitted critical infrastructure information," and raise awareness regarding removal of impediments to information sharing. The office is responsible for receiving, validating, and safeguarding critical information submitted to the DHS. Information submitted, if it satisfies requirements of the PCII Program, is protected from public disclosure under FOIA, State and local Sunshine Laws, and from use in civil litigation. Still, many utilities are not convinced the program can fully protect their sensitive information.

Until the Federal Government can offer reassurance that information pertaining to their individual utility's vulnerabilities and consequences will be protected, utilities will be hesitant to provide this type of information to the government. In addition, should EPA voluntarily collect specific information from the Water Sector, that request will be governed by PRA provisions and will necessitate issuing an Information Collection Request through the Federal Register. To provide and protect information pertaining to its security status and improvements, as envisioned under the NIPP and in the absence of any statutory requirements, the sector must identify mechanisms for providing consequence analysis, vulnerability, and threat information to utilities, and needs to develop a mechanism for collecting, verifying, validating, storing, protecting, and tracking sector priorities and critical infrastructure information to illustrate security progress.

EPA, cooperating with its sector security partners, will work with utilities to identify the necessity and the means for receiving, collecting, and protecting voluntarily submitted, security-related data.

Appendix 1: List of Acronyms and Abbreviations

AMWA	Association of Metropolitan Water Agencies		**CWA**	Clean Water Act
APHL	Association of Public Health Laboratories		**CWNS**	Clean Watersheds Needs Survey
ASDWA	Association of State Drinking Water Administrators		**CWS**	Community Water System
			DHS	Department of Homeland Security
ASIWPCA	Association of State and Interstate Water Pollution Control Administrators		**DoD**	Department of Defense
			DOE	Department of Energy
AWWA	American Water Works Association		**DOT**	Department of Transportation
AwwaRF	American Water Works Association Research Foundation		**DSRC**	Distribution System Research Consortium
BLM	Bureau of Land Management		**ECAT**	Emergency Consequence Assessment Tool
BuRec	Bureau of Reclamation		**EMS**	Emergency Management Services
CBR	Chemical, Biological, or Radiological		**EPA**	U.S. Environmental Protection Agency
CDC	Centers for Disease Control and Prevention		**ERP**	Emergency Response Plan
CERCLA	Comprehensive Environmental Response, Compensation, and Liability Act ("Superfund")		**EWS**	Early Warning System
			FBI	Federal Bureau of Investigation
			FCC	Federal Communications Commission
CFR	Code of Federal Regulations		**FDA**	Food and Drug Administration
CIA	Central Intelligence Agency		**FEMA**	Federal Emergency Management Agency
CII	Critical Infrastructure Information		**FERC**	Federal Energy Regulatory Commission
CI/KR	Critical Infrastructure and Key Resources		**FERN**	Food Emergency Response Network
CIP	Critical Infrastructure Protection		**FOIA**	Freedom of Information Act
CIPAC	Critical Infrastructure Partnership Advisory Council		**FSLC**	Federal Senior Leadership Council
CIP R&D	Critical Infrastructure Protection Research and Development		**GAO**	Government Accountability Office
			GCC	Government Coordinating Council
CMP	Consequence Management Plan		**G&T**	Office of Grants and Training
CSO	Combined Sewer Overflow		**HHS**	Department of Health and Human Services

HITRAC	Homeland Infrastructure Threat and Risk Analysis Center	**PAL**	Provisional Advisory Levels
HSC	Homeland Security Council	**PCII**	Protected Critical Infrastructure Information
HSIN	Homeland Security Information network	**PCS**	Permit Compliance System
HSPD	Homeland Security Presidential Directive	**PDD**	Presidential Decision Directive
ISC	Infrastructure Subcommittee	**POE**	Point-of-Entry
IT	Information Technology	**POTW**	Publicly Owned Treatment Works
LEPC	Local Emergency Planning Committee	**POU**	Point-of-Use
LRN	Laboratory Response Network	**PRA**	Paperwork Reduction Act
MSDS	Material Safety Data Sheet	**PWS**	Public Water System
MTG	Measures Testing Group	**R&D**	Research and Development
NACWA	National Association of Clean Water Agencies	**RAM-W**	Risk Assessment Methodology-Water
NADB	National Asset Database	**RAMCAP**	Risk Analysis and Management for Critical Asset Protection
NAS	National Academy of Sciences	**RCRA**	Resource Conservation and Recovery Act
NAWC	National Association of Water Companies	**RMP**	Risk Management Plan
NCSD	National Cyber Security Division	**S&T**	Science and Technology
NCWS	Non-Community Water System	**SAM**	Standard Analytical Methods
NDWAC	National Drinking Water Advisory Council	**SCADA**	Supervisory Control and Data Acquisition
NHSRC	National Homeland Security Research Center	**SCC**	Sector Coordinating Council
NIPP	National Infrastructure Protection Plan	**SDWA**	Safe Drinking Water Act
NPDES	National Pollutant Discharge Elimination System	**SDWIS**	Safe Drinking Water Information System
NPDN	National Plant Diagnostic Network	**SERC**	State Emergency Response Commission
NPS	National Park Service	**SLTGCC**	State, Local, and Tribal Government Coordinating Council
NRP	National Response Plan	**SSA**	Sector-Specific Agency
NRWA	National Rural Water Association	**SSP**	Sector-Specific Plan
NTNCWS	Non-Transient Non-Community Water System	**TCAD**	Threat Consequence and Analysis Division
O&M	Operations and Maintenance	**TEVA**	Threat Ensemble Vulnerability Assessment
OCA	Off-Site Consequence Analysis	**TNCWS**	Transient Non-Community Water System
OHS	Office of Homeland Security	**TTEP**	Technology Testing and Evaluation Program
OMB	Office of Management and Budget	**USACE**	U.S. Army Corps of Engineers
OSHA	Occupational Safety and Health Administration	**U.S.C.**	United States Code
OSTP	Office of Science and Technology Policy	**USDA**	U.S. Department of Agriculture
OSWER	Office of Solid Waste and Emergency Response	**USGS**	U.S. Geological Survey
OW	Office of Water	**VSAT**	Vulnerability Self-Assessment Tool

WARN	Water-Wastewater Agency Response Networks
WaterISAC	Water Information Sharing and Analysis Center
WaterSC	Water Security Channel
WATR	Water Alliance for Threat Reduction
WEF	Water Environment Federation
WERF	Water Environment Research Foundation
WLA	Water Laboratory Alliance
WSCC	Water Sector Coordinating Council
WSD	Water Security Division
WSWG	Water Security Working Group

Appendix 2: Security-Related Authorities

There are a number of laws and authorities related to homeland security and protection of critical infrastructure information in addition to those described in section 1. They are discussed below.

Safe Drinking Water Act, 42 U.S.C. 300F-300J-26

The general provisions of the SDWA, established in 1974, provide a basis for drinking water security by protecting the quality and underground sources of the water. To protect the quality of public drinking water, EPA establishes national primary and secondary standards. Forty-nine of the 50 States have received primacy from EPA to administer the safe drinking water program. To obtain primacy, States must adopt regulations no less stringent than the Federal government's and meet other conditions, as described below:

- Adopt, and be implementing, procedures for enforcement of State regulations;

- Maintain an inventory of public water systems in the State;

- Have a program to conduct sanitary surveys of systems in the State;

- Have a program to certify laboratories that will analyze water samples required by the regulations, and identify an EPA-certified laboratory that will serve as the State's principal laboratory;

- Have a program to ensure that new or modified systems will be capable of complying with State primary drinking water regulations;

- Have adequate enforcement authority to compel water systems to comply with national primary drinking water regulations, including:

  − Authority to sue in court;

  − Right to enter and inspect water system facilities;

  − Authority to require systems to keep records and release them to the State;

  − Authority to require systems to notify the public of any violation of State requirements; and

  − Authority to assess civil or criminal penalties for violations of State primary drinking water regulations and public notification requirements;

  − Have adequate recordkeeping and reporting requirements;

- Have variance and exemption requirements as stringent as EPA's, if the State chooses to allow variances or exemptions;

- Have an adequate plan to provide for safe drinking water in such emergencies as natural disasters; and

- Have adopted authority to assess administrative penalties for violations of the approved primacy program.

The statute applies to public water systems, which are defined as systems for providing water to the public for human consumption through pipes and other constructed conveyances, including such Federal facilities as military bases and hospitals, and other sites with their own drinking water systems. Drinking water programs most applicable to water security are:

- **State wellhead protection.** This program provides that States establish programs to protect wellhead areas (i.e., the surface and subsurface areas surrounding water wells or well fields supplying a PWS) from contamination.

- **Source water protection.** EPA has developed guidance for States to carry out source water assessment programs. States must delineate the source water areas of all PWSs and identify actual or potential sources of contamination. Program elements include risk reduction (delineation and source inventories), risk ranking and screening (susceptibility analyses), risk management measures (prevention programs), and preparation for unexpected drinking water supply emergencies (contingency planning).

- **Protection of underground sources of drinking water.** EPA has promulgated regulations for State underground injection control programs to prevent injection that endangers drinking water sources.

- **Sanitary surveys.** States conduct regular sanitary surveys of PWSs. A survey entails review of the water system's components, distribution system plans and maps, O&M records, monitoring and sampling plans, and operator certification.

- **Emergency powers.** EPA is authorized to take necessary precautions upon being told that contamination of a PWS or underground water source could present imminent and substantial danger to human health, and the appropriate State and local authorities have not acted to protect the public.

- **Maintaining records and monitoring.** Suppliers of potable water, and others subject to requirements of the SDWA, may be required by the EPA Administrator to maintain records and conduct monitoring.

- **Public water system supervision grant program.** This program helps States implement drinking water programs to protect public health. These grants are used by State program administrators to monitor drinking water quality, conduct sanitary surveys, enforce drinking water standards, and provide technical assistance to local communities.

- **National drinking water standards.** As noted above, EPA is authorized to establish regulations for national primary and secondary drinking water standards to protect the quality of public drinking water. Use of treatment techniques and technologies, in addition to monitoring requirements (see "Maintaining records and monitoring" above), may be mandated by some drinking water regulations. In addition, EPA may establish an interim drinking water standard for a contaminant to address an urgent threat to public health, and it may publish health advisories (which are not regulations) or take other appropriate actions for contaminants not subject to any national primary drinking water regulation.

Homeland Security Act of 2002, Public Law 107-296

This act created the DHS by bringing together a number of independent agencies to analyze intelligence and coordinate security research across government, academia, and the private sector. Provisions encourage partnerships between government and the Water Sector to better protect civilian infrastructure and to create volunteer teams to help local communities respond to attacks on information systems and communication networks. Section 502 requires the Secretary of Homeland Security to provide funds to EPA for homeland security planning, exercises and training, and equipment.

Critical Infrastructure Information Act of 2002

The CII Act defines critical infrastructure information and provides for development of programs to protect such information, particularly information submitted voluntarily. The act also defines information-sharing and analysis organizations.

Under this act, the DHS has created the PCII Program, designed to encourage private industry and others with knowledge about critical infrastructure to share sensitive and proprietary business information with the government. The focus of this program is: (1) analyzing and securing critical infrastructure and protected systems; (2) identifying vulnerabilities and developing risk assessments; and (3) enhancing recovery preparedness measures.

In addition to laws that regulate the Water Sector directly, other environmental laws give EPA authority to take various actions that affect water security. These laws are described below.

Toxic Substances Control Act, 15 U.S.C. 2601-2692

The law addresses risks to public health and the environment from existing and new chemical substances, any of which could be used to contaminate a water supply. It establishes a framework for identifying potentially harmful chemical substances and controlling their use through a variety of regulatory tools. These tools include screening new chemical substances, testing existing substances, labeling and recordkeeping, and restricting activities involving substances that present unreasonable health or environmental risks. The law also gives EPA the authority to address imminent hazards.

Federal Insecticide, Fungicide, and Rodenticide Act, 7 U.S.C. 136, et seq.

The primary focus of the law is to provide Federal control of pesticide distribution, sale, and use. EPA studies the consequences of pesticide use and requires users (farmers, utilities, and others) to register when purchasing pesticides. Users must also take exams for certification as applicators of pesticides.

All pesticides used in the United States must be registered (licensed) by EPA. Registration ensures that pesticides will be properly labeled and will not cause unreasonable harm to the environment if used according to specifications. This law provides authority for EPA to regulate the use of pesticides, including those that could be used to contaminate water supplies.

The following two laws allow EPA to regulate cleanup of a contaminated drinking water or wastewater system and to control disposal of hazardous waste that would be generated as a result.

Comprehensive Environmental Response, Compensation, and Liability Act (CERCLA), as amended (Superfund), 42 U.S.C. 9601-9675

CERCLA provides for cleanup of sites where hazardous substances have been released into the environment, or where there is a substantial threat that they will be released. The law authorizes EPA to clean up and prevent releases of hazardous substances, and to recover costs from parties that may be responsible for a release or threatened release. It gives the President authority to remove hazardous substances, provide for long-term remedial action, and take any other action necessary to protect the public health, welfare, or the environment. It also creates the National Contingency Plan, which establishes the minimum requirements of the hazardous substance response plan, including methods of determining priorities among releases based on relative risk or danger to public health, welfare, or the environment.

Resource Conservation and Recovery Act (RCRA), 42 U.S.C. 6901-6992K, hazardous waste management (subtitle C)

RCRA regulates management and disposal of hazardous and non-hazardous solid waste. Subtitle C establishes a comprehensive system designed to manage hazardous waste from its creation, through its transportation, to its ultimate disposal. RCRA requires EPA to ban injection of certain wastes deep underground as a means to dispose of them if it may be reasonably determined that such disposal may not protect human health and the environment for as long as the waste remains hazardous.

A number of regulations allow the Federal government to identify drinking water and wastewater treatment plants where large quantities of hazardous chemicals are stored, and to reduce the ability of trespassers to obtain access to those chemicals. These regulations include:

Occupational Safety and Health Administration (OSHA) Process Safety Management Rule (29 CFR 1910.119)

Some water utilities that store or use more than 1,500 pounds of gaseous chlorine (or other listed toxic chemicals) are required to comply with this rule. It is designed to prevent or minimize the consequences of catastrophic releases of highly toxic chemicals by requiring facilities to design and operate safe processes and plan for emergencies.

Other OSHA Safety Regulations

Several other important OSHA safety regulations apply to work sites containing such toxic chemicals as chlorine gas. These regulations include the OSHA Hazard Communication Standard (29 CFR 1910.1200), Standard for Control of Hazardous Energy (lockout/tag out) (29 CFR 1910.147), Respiratory Protection Standard (29 CFR 1910.134), Personal Protective Equipment Standard (29 CFR 1910.132), and Hazardous Waste Operations and Emergency Response Standard (29 CFR 1910.120).

Clean Air Act, Section 112(r), 42 U.S.C. 7401-7671q, EPA Risk Management Plan Regulation (40 CFR 68.150)

Utility processes containing more than 2,500 pounds of chlorine gas are required to implement an accident prevention program, conduct a hazard assessment, prepare and implement an ERP, and submit to EPA a summary report known as a risk management plan (RMP). The RMP must include an executive summary that provides a brief description of the facility's accidental release prevention and emergency response policies, the regulated substances handled at the facility, the worst-case release scenario(s) and alternative release scenario(s), the 5-year accident history of the facility, the ERP, and planned changes to improve safety at the facility (see 40 CFR Part 68). The full RMP also includes an Off-Site Consequences Analysis (OCA), which provides the real extent of a worst-case scenario.

Pursuant to the Chemical Safety Information, Site Security and Fuels Regulatory Relief Act (Public Law 106-40), OCA information is no longer made available to the public via the EPA Web Site. However, under the law, Federal reading rooms provide the public with read-only access to paper copies of RMPs, including OCA information submitted by chemical facilities. Other chemicals that may be present at Water Sector utilities, including ammonia, sulfur dioxide, and chlorine dioxide, also trigger RMP regulatory requirements if they exceed certain threshold quantities.

The following acts affect the public's ability to obtain information pertaining to the critical infrastructure of drinking water and wastewater systems.

Emergency Planning and Community Right-To-Know Act, 42 U.S.C. 11001-11050

The law requires States to establish State Emergency Response Commissions (SERCs), which, in turn, are required to establish local emergency planning committees (LEPCs). The LEPCs are to develop local ERPs for releases of extremely hazardous chemicals.

Each facility handling extremely hazardous chemicals in excess of threshold quantities must notify the LEPC and report any releases over a threshold quantity. If the facility is required under the Occupational Safety and Health Act of 1970 (29 U.S.C. 651, et seq.) to maintain material safety data sheets (MSDSs), it must submit an MSDS for each extremely hazardous chemical on site above the threshold quantity, or a list of such chemicals, grouped by hazard (e.g., flammable, toxic), to the LEPC, SERC, and local fire department. The facilities must also submit annual inventories of toxic chemicals managed at the facility over the threshold quantity during the previous year. The information submitted to the LEPC, SERC, and local fire department would be useful to the DHS in identifying at-risk facilities and to determine the mitigation and response measures in place at each facility.

Freedom of Information Act (FOIA), 5 U.S.C. 552-552A

FOIA provides a mechanism for members of the public to obtain documents and other information from Federal agencies. The law exempts from disclosure matters relating to national defense or foreign policy, matters specifically exempted by statute, trade secrets and privileged or confidential commercial matters, inter- and intra-agency memoranda not available by law outside of litigation, certain records or documents compiled for purposes of law enforcement, and other categories of sensitive information. Vulnerability assessments provided to EPA under SDWA section 1433, and any information derived from them, is exempt from disclosure under FOIA.

Federal Advisory Committee Act, 5 U.S.C. 5, Appendix 01/02/01

The purpose of the law is to ensure that advice rendered to the executive branch by the various advisory committees, task forces, boards, and commissions formed by Congress and the President is objective and accessible to the public. Committee memberships must be fairly balanced in terms of the points of view represented and the functions to be performed. Committee meetings must be open to the public, and records of them must be publicly available.

Appendix 3: Protective Program Products and Tools

The following information illustrates the variety of products and tools developed and supported by EPA. A major component of EPA's security program is development of products and tools that support utility protective programs. This is not meant to be a listing of all available tools and programs either initiated or completed by the Agency. These items support the vision and goals of the Water Sector In terms of prevention, detection, response to, and recovery from manmade or naturally occurring events. Since EPA's security program came about before the sector developed its goals and objectives, these items are organized under EPA's security program pillars rather than the sector's security goals and objectives.

Prevention

To prevent or delay an incident, systems typically employ a suite of tools, including enhanced police presence, restricted access, fencing, structural integrity, vehicle checkpoints, and such cyber protection features as additional access controls. In the Water Sector, the asset owner/operators take these measures, which may vary depending on threat level. While many water and wastewater systems already have some protective security elements in place, such as fences, locks, and computer firewalls, previously there was no defined industry standard for these measures, particularly as they relate to protection against a terrorist act. EPA has developed or supported the following tools to assist the sector:

- **Interim Voluntary Security Guidance for Water Utilities.** This provides information to designers and owner/operators of drinking water facilities on design upgrades that improve physical security, and on management and operating practices to reduce vulnerability to malevolent acts. EPA is currently providing training on this guidance.

- **Interim Voluntary Security Guidance for Wastewater Utilities.** This provides information to designers and owner/operators of wastewater/storm water facilities on design upgrades that improve physical security, and on management and operating practices to reduce vulnerability. EPA is currently providing training on this guidance.

- **TEVA Computational Framework.** NHSRC is developing the TEVA program to counter threats against water systems. The program uses a computational framework containing a suite of software tools that can simulate threats, identify vulnerabilities in drinking water distribution systems, measure potential public health impacts, and evaluate mitigation and response strategies.

- **Top Ten List for Small Ground Water Suppliers.** This list was developed by EPA's New England office to assist small PWSs with security and emergency planning. It includes tips to help suppliers protect their facilities from tampering or contamination, and to prepare for potential emergencies. A similar list is being developed for wastewater systems.

- **Guarding Against Terrorist and Security Threats.** These documents for drinking water and wastewater utilities describe the protective steps that systems should take under the DHS's five-tiered homeland security advisory system. Actions for detection, preparedness, prevention, and protection are provided for each threat-level color: green, blue, yellow, orange, and red.

- **Security Products Guide.** This series of guides assists water treatment plant operators and utility managers in reducing risks from, and providing protection against, possible natural disasters and intentional terrorist attacks. The guides are available on EPA's security Web site. They provide information on a variety of products available to enhance physical security (including monitoring tools) and electronic or cyber security. The Web site is updated as new information and technologies become available. A feedback page enables users to comment on the materials. Several products will help utilities prevent or delay potential adversaries, as well as detect incidents.

- **Point of Use/Point of Entry Devices for Water System Protection.** Point-of-Use (POU) and Point-of-Entry (POE) devices can proactively protect a water system against contamination; they can be used as a response measure when a water system becomes contaminated, and can be used to identify contaminants introduced into a system. As part of TTEP, EPA is identifying POU and POE devices, their uses, and disposal requirements.

Recognizing the Water Sector's dependency on other sectors and stakeholders, EPA also developed or supported a number of outreach materials for the public, law enforcement, and medical community to increase their awareness of sector security issues, which are as follows:

- **Water Watchers: We Are All in This Together (EPA 810-F-03-006).** A brochure for residents that describes how they can help local authorities protect the water utilities in their communities.

- **Water Security and You.** A drop-in article for local news media that describes examples of suspicious activity.

- **Top Ten List:** *Water Supply Emergency Preparedness and Security for Law Enforcement* **(EPA 901-H-03-002).** A poster for display in local municipal facilities to aid coordination between law enforcement, the water supply industry, and public health officials.

- **Top Ten List Visor Card for Law Enforcement (EPA 817-F-03-003).** A visor card version of the above flyer.

- **Drinking Water Security, Report Suspicious Activities.** A series of four flyers for display in local municipal, recreational, and commercial buildings to encourage citizens to watch out for and report suspicious activity around water resources, water structures, and equipment.

- **Water Security Progress and Resources (EPA 817-F-03-001).** A four-page flyer highlighting the achievements and ongoing projects of the Water Sector security program and its partners.

- **Recognizing Waterborne Disease and the Health Effects of Water Pollution: A Physician's On-Line Reference Guide.** A Web-based educational tool to help health care providers recognize and manage waterborne disease outbreaks and the health effects of natural or intentional contamination of water. Features of the Web site include availability 24 hours per day, 7 days per week, with free access; clinically relevant information detailing the diagnosis and management of waterborne disease; and a repository of physician antiterrorism preparedness resources.

Detection

To detect an incident, systems typically rely on intrusion detection systems, monitoring, operation alarms, and employee security awareness programs. These actions are taken at the asset level by the Water Sector. Examples of some of the programs and tools developed to support detection activities are outlined below.

- **Riverspill.** A geographical information systems-based method to track and model the flow and concentration of contaminants in source water supplies, Riverspill simulates downstream movement of a contaminant plume in a river or river-reservoir system, including travel time and changes in concentration. It also identifies drinking water systems that would be impacted by introduction of contaminants at PWSs. USGS has more data regarding flow characteristics, as the modeling issues are complex.

- **PipelineNet.** This software program monitors and projects the fate and transport of contaminants potentially introduced into water distribution systems, particularly as related to use and application in an emergency. It can be used to determine optimal placement of extraction and monitoring instruments, to help develop monitoring regimes for routine screening of distribution system water quality, and predict and track the fate and transport of contaminants in a system in order to effectively respond to purposeful contamination and such accidental events as backflows or cross connections. The software is available at http://eh2o.saic.com/iwqss.

- **Technology Testing and Evaluation Program.** EPA's NHSRC, headquartered in Cincinnati, Ohio, has developed the Technology Testing and Evaluation Program (TTEP) to provide reliable information on performance of homeland security-related technologies. TTEP is an outgrowth of EPA's successful and internationally recognized Environmental Technology Verification Program. The technology categories of interest include detection, monitoring, treatment, decontamination, computer modeling, and design tools for use by those responsible for protecting water infrastructure and decontaminating structures and the outdoor environment. For more details, visit www.epa.gov/nhsrc.

Response and Recovery

Historically the Water Sector has been prepared to respond to and recover from such natural disasters as hurricanes, floods, and earthquakes. This includes coordination of first-responders, State public health and environmental officials, State National Guard, and, when necessary, support from FEMA and other Federal agencies. Many water and wastewater utilities rely on ERPs to prepare for and respond to these disasters. These plans are updated periodically by the utilities and typically are reviewed by State primacy agencies and permitting authorities during site inspections. From a security standpoint, ERPs are critical for systems unable to sufficiently harden vulnerable targets or when security efforts fail. The Bioterrorism Act requires that drinking water utilities serving more than 3,300 people prepare or revise ERPs to incorporate the results of completed vulnerability assessments. In addition to ERPs, drinking water and wastewater systems may have other programs in place, including:

- RMPs;

- Source-water assessment and protection plans;

- Watershed protection plans;

- Cross-connection control plans; and

- Communications and outreach plans.

The Water Sector encourages utilities to coordinate their activities with their county LEPCs. The committees are created by State emergency response commissions under the Emergency Planning Community Right-to-Know Act; their members are drawn from public safety, health care, and local industry. They are required to submit ERPs to their SERCs that identify hazardous chemical storage and transportation, and procedures for emergency response, public notification, and evacuation in case of an accidental release, spill, or other chemical emergency. The tools, guidelines, and training that EPA has developed to help utilities develop and enhance their ERPs include:

- **Water Alliance for Threat Reduction (WATR).** EPA created WATR to further help utilities prepare, prevent, and respond to contamination or other intentional events. Utilities, emergency responders, and decision makers will be trained to evaluate and respond effectively to water threats and incidents, and will receive technical assistance and training on implementing active and effective security programs. Additional emergency response tools will be developed that include information on high-priority contaminants, sampling and detection methods, and treatment options.

- **Water Contaminant Information Tool.** The tool is a secure, online database under development by EPA that will provide information on contaminants of concern for water security. As a planning tool, it can help create and update vulnerability assessments, ERPs, and site-specific response guidelines. As a response tool, it can provide real-time data on water contaminants to help first-responders and utilities make better decisions.

- **Chemical and Biological Helpline Database.** The Chemical and Biological Helpline database provides information on general policy, training, and equipment needed to plan and train for homeland security incidents. The database contains sensitive information on detecting and obviating contaminants, specifications for chemical and biological equipment, and instructions on advisories and other procedures. Medical data includes information on recognizing exposure symptoms, providing proper medical treatment, and obtaining protective equipment. NHSRC, in conjunction with the U.S. Army Edgewood Chemical and Biological Center, is modifying the database to include laboratory analytical methods.

- **Emergency Consequence Assessment Tool (ECAT).** The objective of this project is to develop the prototype and enhancements for a secure, Web-based risk tool that will make risk assessment and consequence management faster and easier for high-priority threat scenarios. ECAT has been designed as a response template enabling first-responders, health advisors, and emergency management officials to have access to critical information for responding to a terrorist attack or natural disaster. An innovative feature of ECAT is that it organizes key information using both the emergency response paradigm and risk assessment paradigm. The prototype version 2.0 of ECAT currently addresses 11 priority threat scenarios. The next generation of ECAT will have significant enhancements, including a greatly expanded number of chemical/biological agents (more than 100); many more threat scenarios (100-plus), as well as expansion of several threat scenarios. ECAT will include hyperlinks to more extensive databases and models for each element of the risk assessment paradigm. It will serve as a repository or online library for many products in NHSRC, thus allowing one-stop shopping for key information.

- **National Environmental Laboratory Network.** EPA is funding development of the network to enhance the capacity and capability of environmental laboratories to respond to emergencies and potential terrorist acts. The goal is to maximize laboratory capacity to handle a surge in environmental samples, develop water and general environmental laboratory methods, and facilitate development/dissemination of tools to increase laboratory effectiveness.

- **E-Plan HazMat Response System.** E-Plan is a Web-based system that assembles facility-specific hazard information from numerous sources. The foundation of E-Plan is EPA's Tier II "Right-to-Know" reporting requirements. It has been expanded to include four additional databases: 24-hour contact information, site and building plans, chemical inventories, and MSDSs for hundreds more facilities.

- **Standard Analytical Methods (SAM).** NHSRC, in conjunction with EPA's Laboratory Capacity and Capability Committee, has developed a list, SAM, to be used by environmental laboratories in analyzing biological and chemical samples associated with threats to homeland security. SAM currently contains procedures to identify and measure approximately 120 priority contaminants that could be used in future terrorist attacks.

- **Message Mapping Communication Tool.** "Message mapping" is a science-based risk communication tool. The purpose of the tool is to train scientists, first-responders, public information officers, and others to communicate using message-mapping techniques during high-stress situations, such as disasters and terrorist incidents; and to develop scientifically sound message maps for a variety of potential homeland security incidents. The training and message map development will occur through a series of workshops attended by multi-jurisdictional, multidisciplinary subject matter experts. To date, message maps have been developed for seven scenarios affecting drinking water: (1) a contagious biological agent in the water; (2)

a physical attack on the drinking water distribution system; (3) receipt of a credible note threatening the drinking water supply; (4) the impact of massive power failure on drinking water distribution; (5) an infectious but not contagious biological agent in the water; (6) drinking water contamination with a fast-acting pesticide; and (7) drinking water contamination with a chemical warfare agent.

- **Compilation of Toxicity Values for Priority Threat Agents.** The objective of this effort is to develop a "data dictionary" of compiled primary and secondary data for a priority list of CBR contaminants. The dictionary will be a compilation of toxicity and infectivity data, risk assessment methods, dose-response, and health effects information for chemical agents (warfare agents, toxic industrial chemicals) and biological agents of concern related to homeland security issues. Information on bio-aerosols, secondary disease transmission, and decontamination byproducts will also be compiled. The data presented in the dictionary will be used for other analyses in the Threat Consequence and Analysis Division (TCAD) and by other NHSRC divisions, and as inputs to numerous activities and products such as fact sheets, derivation of provisional advisory levels, development of rapid risk tools, ECAT, and the TEVA modeling tool. This information will be used by NHSRC scientists and engineers to help make rapid decisions pertaining to containment, treatment, decontamination, and disposal of contaminated media. TCAD is partnering with DOE's Argonne National Laboratory and the Chemical and Biological Information Analysis Center to conduct this research.

- **Large Water System Emergency Response Plan Outline: Guidance to Assist Community Water Systems in Complying with the Public Health Security and Bioterrorism Preparedness and Response Act of 2002.** This document was developed to help utilities prepare ERPs as required by the Bioterrorism Act.

- **Emergency Response Plan Guidance for Small and Medium Drinking Water Systems (EPA 816-R-04-002).** A document for CWSs serving populations of 3,301 to 99,999, to develop or revise ERPs. The document is of value to key authorities with critical roles during emergency response or remediation actions concerning a drinking-water contamination threat or incident. Printed copies, in limited quantity, can be obtained from the National Service Center for Environmental Publications. A similar guide is under development for wastewater systems.

- **Wastewater Emergency Response Plan Guidance.** This document is intended to help wastewater systems of all sizes organize planning efforts, and to be a reference for the types of information and data that should be included in ERPs.

- **Response Protocol Toolbox: Planning for and Responding to Contamination Threats to Drinking Water Systems.** This interim final toolbox is designed to help the Water Sector effectively and appropriately respond to intentional contamination threats and incidents. EPA, building on the experience and expertise of several drinking water utilities, produced the toolbox. Organized in modular format, the toolbox is of value to drinking water utilities, laboratories, emergency responders, State drinking water programs, technical assistance providers, and public health and law enforcement officials. A similar tool is being developed for wastewater systems. The toolbox contains the modules described below.

- **Overview of the Response Protocol Toolbox (EPA-817-D-03-007).** Provides an overview of the modules contained in the toolbox.

- **Water Utility Planning Guide: Module 1 (EPA-817-D-03-001).** Provides a brief discussion of the nature of the contamination threat to the water supply, and describes the planning activities that a utility may undertake to ready a response to contamination threats and incidents.

- **Contamination Threat Management Guide: Module 2 (EPA-817-D-03-002).** Presents the overarching framework for management of contamination threats to drinking water supplies. The guide involves evaluating the threat and making decisions on appropriate actions in response to the threat.

- **Site Characterization and Sampling Guide: Module 3 (EPA-817-D-03-003).** Describes the site characterization process-information is gathered at a suspected contamination incident at a drinking water system, including site investigation, field safety screening, rapid field-testing of water, and sample collection.

- **Analytical Guide: Module 4 (EPA-817-D-03-004).** Presents an approach to analysis of samples collected from the site of a suspected contamination incident.

- **Public Health Response Guide: Module 5 (EPA-817-D-03-005).** Addresses the public health response measures that could be used to minimize public exposure to potentially contaminated water. The guide examines the role of the utility during a public health response action, and the interactions among the utility, drinking water primacy agency, public health community, and others.

- **Remediation and Recovery Guide: Module 6 (EPA-817-D-03-006).** Describes the planning and implementation of necessary remediation and recovery activities following a confirmed contamination incident, including system characterization, selection of remedy options, provision of alternative water, and monitoring to demonstrate that the system has been remediated. This module describes the roles of the utility and other response organizations.

- **EPA Environmental Laboratory Compendium.** This compendium is a database of environmental laboratories available to water utilities and Federal and State agencies. It contains laboratory-specific capabilities and capacities to analyze chemical and biological analytes, as well as chemical warfare, bioterrorism, and radiochemical agents. It was developed to quickly identify laboratories with capabilities to support incident-specific response and recovery. The compendium is intended to serve water utilities and Federal and State agencies in responding to contamination threats, terrorist attacks, or natural disasters.

Training in the use of the vulnerability assessment tools, development of ERPs, and general security issues, has been and continues to be provided, using a number of Water Sector organizations. Many States worked with local affiliates of the national Water Sector organizations to target security training for their utilities. Example training and tools are described below.

- **Emergency Response Tabletop CD-ROM Exercises for Drinking Water and Wastewater Systems (EPA-817-C-05-001).** The CD-based tool contains tabletop exercises to help train water and wastewater utility workers in preparing and carrying out ERPs. The exercises provided on the CD can help strengthen relationships between a water supplier and their emergency response team (e.g., health officials; laboratories; fire; police; emergency medical services; and local, State, and Federal officials). Users can also adapt the materials for their own needs. Users can choose from five basic event types: intentional contamination, security breach, cyber security, physical attack, and interdependency. The exercises also allow water suppliers to test their ERPs before an actual incident occurs.

- **Water Security Awareness Training for Law Enforcement.** Workshops for representatives of the FBI's Joint Terrorism Task Force provide an understanding of water systems, their vulnerabilities and current threats, and appropriate responses. A drinking water or wastewater system's ERP should outline the steps to bring the system back online after an incident. These steps include ensuring that the contamination has been properly addressed, and communicating with the public. EPA's Water Security Research and Technical Action Plan contains a number of research initiatives related to decontamination and recovery.

- **Decision Support Tool for Disposal of Contaminated Building and Water Systems Materials.** A vital part of the contaminated site restoration process includes decisions related to treatment or disposal, selection of disposal facilities, transporting materials, worker safety, and protecting human health and the environment. To assist in this area, NHSRC is developing a Web-based decision support tool for disposal of residuals from decontamination of buildings and water systems.

- **Planning for Decontamination Wastewater: A Guide for Utilities.** NACWA developed this guide to help utilities understand and reduce the risks associated with decontamination wastewater that may contain chemical and biological warfare agents, radioactive materials, and chemicals used in the decontamination process. The guide is designed to help wastewater utility managers take the necessary preplanning steps to deal with such an event.

Appendix 4: Outreach and Communication Mechanisms

EPA and its sector security partners continue to maintain and develop outreach forums and modes of communication to help better protect critical Water Sector infrastructure. Examples follow:

- **Web sites.** EPA maintains several comprehensive Web sites. These include sites for the drinking water program (www.epa.gov/safewater), wastewater program (www.epa.gov/owm), Water Sector security program (www.epa.gov/safewater/security/index.html), and NHSRC (www.epa.gov/ordnhsrc). These Web sites provide access to all governing authorities and directives, and contain detailed information about training, vulnerability assessment tools, emergency response tools, technical and financial assistance, information sharing, research, outreach documents, a security products guide, and other links.

- **Partner updates.** EPA holds regular conference calls as needed, but typically on a monthly schedule, and quarterly face-to-face meetings with sector security partners to provide updates on security initiatives. In addition to the organizations listed above, participants include organizations that represent governors and State drinking water and wastewater programs, county and city health officials, training centers, equipment manufacturers and their organizations, public works and infrastructure organizations, and other Federal agencies.

- **E-mail trees.** EPA and sector security partners have developed e-mail trees of partner organizations and utilities that permit rapid communication of late-breaking news and information. These partners, in turn, share the information with their constituencies, which include thousands of drinking water and wastewater utilities.

- **Newsletters.** Many national Water Sector and State associations have created security newsletters to provide regular updates to their constituents.

- **Web casts and conferences.** Many national Water Sector and State associations have provided security-related Web casts, and have participated in regional and national conferences; EPA has also been involved with aspects of these activities.

- **Training.** EPA funds a number of organizations to provide training on vulnerability assessment tools, emergency response protocols, and general security training. These training sessions are directed at utility owner/operators.

- **Stakeholder Engagement.** EPA seeks input from its sector security partners in development and review of security-related products and discussion of security issues. In addition to numerous meetings with individual partner organizations and their members, in 2005 WEF, working with EPA, hosted three Water Sector Security Workshops. Approximately 300 representatives participated in one of the three workshops. A major goal was to ensure a balance of interests among the sector, including all size urban and rural utilities and other appropriate stakeholders. During the workshops, three overarching challenges emerged, including: (1) maintaining support in security investments, (2) addressing the vulnerability of utility distribution systems, and (3) managing sector security information. A number of application and research needs were also identified. The WSSC played an essential role in planning and implementing the workshops along with numerous sector security partners. A final report on these findings was released in 2006 and can be accessed at either EPA's or WEF's Web site.

- **The Infrastructure Security Partnership.** To reach additional private sector stakeholders, EPA is working with an organization of associations providing technical support to the security of the Nation's built environment. The partnership's fundamental goal is to reach and include all stakeholders potentially impacted by any disaster, and to provide technical assistance and information to the DHS.

- **Distribution System Research Consortium.** NHSRC created this group, composed of EPA and Federal and nongovernmental partners. It interacts with academia and industry through five technical working groups. The Consortium, which meets periodically, is dedicated to the advancement of science, technology, and research to protect drinking water distribution systems from terrorist threats and attacks.

- **State Primacy Agencies and Permitting Authorities.** Because of the large number of small drinking water and wastewater systems, EPA is also working through State primacy agencies and permitting authorities to develop communication vehicles and networks at the State and local levels to deal directly with them on security issues.

- **Public Service Information.** The general public is an important partner in the Water Sector's security activities. EPA and its sector security partners have included security-related public service information on their Web sites, developed security flyers and outreach materials for the public and encouraged utilities to use the public as additional eyes and ears to report suspicious activities.